Understanding and Supporting Pupils with Moderate Learning Difficulties in the Secondary School

Are you working with students who have Moderate Learning Difficulties?

Do you want to know how best to help them?

Are you confused about what helps and what hinders?

Learners with MLD form one of the largest categories of special educational needs in mainstream secondary schools. In most schools, the vast majority of learners with MLD will be taught in mainstream classes much of the time. This book outlines a range of strategies and approaches for supporting these learners, with key points covering:

- definitions and identification of MLD;
- teaching strategies and approaches;
- developing key conceptual, literacy and social skills;
- effective support from your Teaching Assistant;
- theoretical perspectives on learning.

Understanding and Supporting Pupils with Moderate Learning Difficulties in the Secondary School provides an introduction to a wide range of ideas, arguments and perspectives about ways of understanding and supporting learners who are considered to have MLD. This is a much-needed source of knowledge for teachers, TAs, SENCos, learning mentors and anyone who supports children and young people with MLD and provides an honest and accessible approach.

Rachael Hayes is an educational psychologist with experience of working in primary schools, secondary schools and Pupil Referral Units.

Pippa Whittaker is a SENCo who has worked in four secondary schools to date. She is currently Curriculum Leader for Inclusion in a large and diverse inner-city academy.

nasen is a professional membership association that supports all those who work with or care for children and young people with special and additional educational needs. Members include teachers, teaching assistants, support workers, other educationalists, students and parents.

nasen supports its members through policy documents, journals, its magazine *Special!*, publications, professional development courses, regional networks and newsletters. Its website contains more current information such as responses to government consultations. **nasen**'s published documents are held in very high regard both in the UK and internationally.

Other titles published in association with the National Association for Special Educational Needs (nasen):

Language for Learning in the Secondary School: A Practical Guide for Supporting Students with Speech, Language and Communication Needs
Sue Hayden and Emma Jordan
2012/pb: 978-0-415-61975-2

Using Playful Practice to Communicate with Special Children
Margaret Corke
2012/pb: 978-0-415-68767-6

The Equality Act for Educational Professionals: A Simple Guide to Disability and Inclusion in Schools
Geraldine Hills
2012/pb: 978-0-415-68768-3

More Trouble with Maths: A Teacher's Complete Guide to Identifying and Diagnosing Mathematical Difficulties
Steve Chinn
2012/pb: 978-0-415-67013-5

Dyslexia and Inclusion: Classroom Approaches for Assessment, Teaching and Learning, Second Edition
Gavin Reid
2012/pb: 978-0-415-60758-2

Provision Mapping: Improving Outcomes in Primary Schools
Anne Massey
2012/pb: 978-0-415-53030-9

Beating Bureaucracy in Special Educational Needs: Helping SENCOs Maintain a Work/Life Balance, Second Edition
Jean Gross
2012/pb: 978-0-415-53374-4

Promoting and Delivering School-to-School Support for Special Educational Needs: A Practical Guide for SENCOs
Rita Cheminais
2013/pb: 978-0-415-63370-3

Time to Talk: Implementing Outstanding Practice in Speech, Language and Communication
Jean Gross
2013/pb: 978-0-415-63334-5

Curricula for Teaching Children and Young People with Severe or Profound and Multiple Learning Difficulties: Practical strategies for educational professionals
Peter Imray and Viv Hinchcliffe
2013/pb: 978-0-415-83847-4

Successfully Managing ADHD: A handbook for SENCOs and teachers
Fintan O'Regan
2014/pb: 978-0-415-59770-8

Brilliant Ideas for Using ICT in the Inclusive Classroom, second edition
Sally McKeown and Angela McGlashon
2015/pb: 978-1-138-80902-4

Boosting Learning in the Primary Classroom: Occupational therapy strategies that really work with pupils
Sheilagh Blyth
2015/pb: 978-1-13-882678-6

Beating Bureaucracy in Special Educational Needs, third edition
Jean Gross
2015/pb: 978-1-138-89171-5

Transforming Reading Skills in the Secondary School: Simple strategies for improving literacy
Pat Guy
2016/pb: 978-1-138-89272-9

Developing Memory Skills in the Primary Classroom: A complete programme for all
Gill Davies
2016/pb: 978-1-138-89262-0

Language for Learning in the Primary School: A practical guide for supporting pupils with language and communication difficulties across the curriculum, second edition
Sue Hayden and Emma Jordan
2015/pb: 978-1-138-89862-2

Understanding and Supporting Pupils with Moderate Learning Difficulties in the Secondary School: A practical guide
Rachael Hayes and Pippa Whittaker
2016/pb: 978-1-138-01910-2

Assessing Children with Specific Learning Difficulties: A teacher's practical guide
Gavin Reid, Gad Elbeheri and John Everatt
2016/pb: 978-0-415-67027-2

Understanding and Supporting Pupils with Moderate Learning Difficulties in the Secondary School

A practical guide

Rachael Hayes and Pippa Whittaker

Routledge
Taylor & Francis Group

LONDON AND NEW YORK

First published 2016
by Routledge
2 Park Square, Milton Park, Abingdon, Oxon OX14 4RN

and by Routledge
711 Third Avenue, New York, NY 10017

Routledge is an imprint of the Taylor & Francis Group, an informa business

British Library Cataloguing in Publication Data
A catalogue record for this book is available from the British Library

Library of Congress Cataloging-in-Publication Data
Hayes, Rachael.
Understanding and supporting pupils with moderate learning difficulties in the secondary school : a practical guide / Rachael Hayes and Pippa Whittaker.
pages cm
ISBN 978-1-138-01909-6 (hardback) -- ISBN 978-1-138-01910-2 (pbk.) --
ISBN 978-1-315-77915-7 (e-book) 1. Learning disabled children--Education. I. Whittaker, Pippa. II. Title.
LC4704.H397 2016
371.9--dc23
2015003885

ISBN: 978-1-138-01909-6 (hbk)
ISBN: 978-1-138-01910-2 (pbk)
ISBN: 978-1-315-77915-7 (ebk)

Typeset in Sabon
by Saxon Graphics Ltd, Derby
Printed and bound in Great Britain by Ashford Colour Press Ltd.

Contents

Figures

Introduction

If you have chosen to read this book, then it is very likely that you teach or support learners who have learning difficulties. You will be aware of learners that you work with who have Moderate Learning Difficulties (MLD) as their category of need, and will be looking for clear and practical ways to meet their needs in school. We hope that this book will provide some useful strategies, perspectives and stimulus that will help you to develop great practice for learners with MLD.

Learners with MLD form one of the largest categories of special educational need in mainstream secondary schools, and at the time of writing around one in five learners with significant SEN were identified as having MLD as their primary category of need. In most schools, the vast majority of learners with MLD will be taught in mainstream classes much of the time. In spite of this, there has been far less written about the needs of this group of learners than about other groups, such as those with autism or dyslexia, for example. This book will provide a useful starting point for anyone wanting to better understand the needs of the large number of learners who have MLD. In addition, this guide will support teachers and SENCos to meet the requirements of the new SEND Code of Practice 2014.

Whatever your role might be, you will have undoubtedly already have developed strategies and approaches which work very well with some learners. You will also have come up against difficulties and barriers which persist, in spite of your very best efforts.

One thing you will certainly have noticed is the fact that every learner you work with is different – regardless of which 'label' or 'category' they may have been assigned. Every learner has his or her own character, interests, obsessions, sense of humour, quirks, areas of strength and areas of difficulty. They are individuals and this means their needs can vary on a day-to-day basis. Therefore, their support needs to be flexible and we need to constantly reflect on what they need in each lesson.

Knowing how best to help learners learn is a complex, skilled and subtle business. The key features of any effective and person-centred support must be:

- having a level of sensitive and ongoing communication with the learner;
- testing out your ideas about what might help, and reflecting on the result;
- establishing a positive and constructive relationship with the learner.

Furthermore, it is vital that you use your own emotional intelligence to guide you in recognising and reading the messages from your learners; this might include their feelings about school, learning, curriculum subjects, their social world, and life outside and beyond school. These features are important aspects of all good work with learners, but are even more critical when the learners in question have special educational needs or disabilities.

We take the view that the very best work we can do with our learners comes from a state of open-mindedness, flexibility and reflection. There are no easy answers that will 'solve' a learner's difficulties – the learners we work with are often far too brilliantly unique and complex for that! The aim of this book is, rather, to provide an introduction to a wide range of ideas, arguments and perspectives about ways of understanding and supporting learners who are considered to have MLD. In doing so we hope that the questions you feel yourself asking most frequently are answered. We also hope that this will provide a useful starting point for an intelligent and reflective approach which allows the voice of learners to emerge at its core.

Chapter 1

What is MLD and why does it matter?

The background and context to MLD

MLD is one of the most common categories of SEN in mainstream schools. The DFE Statistical First Release for Special Educational Needs (2014) found that of learners who had SEN at School Action Plus or with Statements in secondary schools, 20.3 per cent had MLD as their primary category of need. The situation in primary schools was very similar with 19.1 per cent having MLD as their primary category of need.

Earlier data (which also included learners at School Action) has suggested that MLD is in fact the greatest category of need when learners at School Action are also taken into account; for example, in 2010 OFSTED found that 24.2 per cent of all learners with SEN had MLD as their main need.

In spite of this evidence on the prevalence of MLD, and the large numbers of learners in our schools who have MLD, many people are far less familiar with MLD than they are with other needs such as autism and dyslexia.

There are a number of reasons why this might be the case. One reason might be that there is little shared agreement about what MLD actually is. For example, there has been discussion about whether learners with MLD might have an identifiable organic impairment – something that exists 'within child' which affects their ability to learn (for example, a neurological difference which affects their memory system) or whether they are learners who are simply working at a lower level than others – sometimes referred to as 'low attainers'. In fact, much of the research on MLD in recent years has focused on trying to define what the term MLD actually means. This has resulted in an inconsistent evidence base to build upon, since researchers' definitions have tended to vary greatly, both in the UK and internationally.

In addition to this, where schools are provided with definitions of MLD, these tend to be broad. The new SEND Code of Practice (2014) provides only a brief mention of MLD within the broader area of Cognition and Learning, and emphasises that it is the assessment of the range of a learner's needs and difficulties which is most important, along with ensuring that planning is in place for these needs.

One of the most useful and accessible definitions of MLD was provided to schools in 2003 by the DfES:

> Pupils with moderate learning difficulties will have attainments well below expected levels in all or most areas of the curriculum, despite appropriate interventions. Their needs will not be able to be met by normal differentiation and the flexibilities of the National Curriculum.

Pupils with MLD have much greater difficulty than their peers in acquiring basic literacy and numeracy skills and in understanding concepts. They may also have associated speech and language delay, low self-esteem, low levels of concentration and under-developed social skills.

(DfES 2003, p. 4)

Many staff who support learners with MLD will recognise these descriptions, and in that sense this may seem a reasonable and usable definition. It continues to be one of the most commonly used definitions in British schools and professional organisations. For these reasons, this is the definition which we will use as our starting point for this book and for the strategies contained within it.

However, it is important, when working with this definition (or indeed any definition), that we are mindful of its limitations. It does not, for example, help us to understand the causes of these difficulties, nor does it explain what an 'appropriate intervention' might be, nor what is considered to be 'normal differentiation'. Some might argue that this definition is too subjective to provide any basis for standardised identification of learners who have a MLD, especially as their difficulties could derive from biological or context-dependent factors.

One factor which can further complicate our understanding of MLD is that there are many reasons why a learner might be considered to have a MLD. For example, there are some children whose learning difficulties are the result of some kind of 'within child' impairment – such as brain damage, for example. However, there are other learners whose learning difficulties might be considered to be the result of their circumstances and upbringing, as research would suggest that a lack of exposure to stimulation, experience, warmth and language have a significant impact on a child's ability to learn and to make links.

This leads us to consider whether learners whose learning difficulties have arisen from different causes need different approaches, and if so, what these might be. We might also wonder who should be making the decision as to whether a learner has MLD – is this a decision for Educational Psychologists, Paediatricians and Specialist Advisory Teachers? Or can a difficulty with learning be best identified by those who know the learner and their learning context – their parents and the staff who work with them in school, perhaps? Should MLD be defined by a comparison to their peers? Or should slow progress be the primary indicator? Or should we be talking about a diagnosable cognitive difficulty? Or a combination of all these factors? If it is a diagnosable difficulty, then what should this diagnosis comprise, and how can we make sure that it is not a simple label, but a detailed description of the learner's strengths and weaknesses taking their environment and background into account? There are so many questions that we might usefully want to ask.

What is certainly clear is that this definition (and many attempts to define difficulties such as MLD) end up raising more questions than it answers. This means that in many cases school staff ultimately do need to work with families to make their own 'best judgement' as to whether a learner meets the criteria for MLD and why. There will be learners for whom this is decided by, for example, an Educational Psychologist or a Specialist Advisory Teacher, but in many cases the majority of learners who meet these descriptors will have been identified by conversations with parents and carers, and by observation and assessment within school, carried out by class teachers, SENCos and TAs.

Another challenge of the MLD 'label' is that it is so open to interpretation – what is considered to be 'greater difficulty than their peers' in a school with a socio-economically privileged intake is likely to be very different to that in a school in an area of significant hardship and deprivation. Similarly, schools that are trying to reduce the number of learners on their SEN register in order to target resources to the most significant areas of need may be less inclined to identify learners with learning difficulties, and the opposite of this is also true.

All in all, this means that these can be great variety in who is considered to have MLD. In schools, the number of learners who are given the MLD 'label' can depend upon the following factors:

- The extra resources and funding that are available for learners with MLD – is there anything, in practical terms, to be gained by designating a learner as having 'MLD' as opposed to just seeing them as a low attainer?
- The level of learners in the school or class as a whole. In a cohort of learners with general low ability (many of whom might meet the criteria for MLD), any one individual is less likely to 'stand out' as having a learning difficulty.
- The desire of parents and professionals to designate learners as having MLD – this can be affected by a broad range of factors, including social stigma or alternatively the quest for a diagnostic label; the need to 'excuse' poor teaching or inadequate differentiation meaning that learners are not making progress.

Of course, you could quite reasonably ask whether being considered to have MLD, as opposed to being considered as a low attaining student, has any benefit for the learner. Research on this point shows that educational outcomes such as progress and qualifications gained are actually very similar for those who are classified as having learning difficulties and disabilities, and those who are classified simply as 'low achievers' (see, for example, Ysseldyke et al. 2001).

In spite of this, a lot has been written in recent years about the need to differentiate between underachieving learners – those for whom expectations have been too low and unambitious targets have been set – and those who have a 'genuine' learning difficulty. This issue was highlighted in 2010 when the OFSTED *Special Educational Needs and Disability Review* reported that 'around half the schools … used low attainment and relatively slow progress as their principal indicators of a special educational need. In nearly a fifth of these cases, there was very little further assessment' (OFSTED 2010, p. 9).

This focus on slow progress provides a contrast with previous government guidance which provides low attainment and difficulty in acquiring concepts as descriptors for MLD. OFSTED does not provide any further guidance as to what the further assessment might include, and what other indicators it believes should be used if not low attainment and slow progress relative to peers. However, the findings of this review do seem to imply that 'genuine' learning difficulties will have a diagnosable biological component, rather than those difficulties which are identified and assessed based on how the child presents and makes progress within their own particular setting and environment.

There remains, therefore, in the UK in particular, a very real lack of clarity about the key denoting factors of MLD. Norwich and Kelly (2005) note that 'children in this area of SEN do not have a clear identity', which might not be considered surprising when all of the above points are taken into account.

Some researchers have tried to resolve these confusions by using different terminology for learning difficulties which have differing causes. For example, some have differentiated between learning difficulties (many of which are created by deficiencies in the social, physical, familial or academic environment), and intellectual disabilities, which are an 'impaired ability to learn' (Westwood 2004, p. 133). However, internationally a range of terms are used interchangeably or to denote overlapping groups of learners, which makes comparative study difficult.

The fact that definitions of MLD are so contradictory and unclear can be seen as both a difficulty and a strength. It is certainly true that this lack of clarity has proved a barrier to developing research and practice in this field – if there is no agreement on what MLD actually is, how can we find out what helps those learners who we consider to have MLD? Nevertheless, there are shared strands of understanding of MLD that have arisen from the research base, which can be usefully explored in further detail. One of these relates to the way in which experience and upbringing can impact upon someone's capacity to learn well – the environmental factors that we mentioned earlier. For many of us working with learners in mainstream schools, this is one of the most pertinent factors to consider when we attempt to develop our own understanding of an individual learner we are working with, and the difficulties they may be facing.

Environmental factors – nature or nurture?

Many researchers have noted that a large proportion of learners identified as having MLD are from lower socio-economic backgrounds (see, for example, Norwich and Kelly 2005, p. 3). There are a number of possible reasons why this might be the case.

We referred earlier to the distinction that is sometimes made between difficulties which are 'within child' (nature) and 'outside child' (nurture). However, the more complex reality is that a learner's brain develops in response to the stimulus it gets from his or her environment – and in this sense, over time, nurture *becomes* nature.

For example, a learner who has been raised in a socio-economically deprived environment, and who has perhaps experienced limited exposure to language in early childhood, may well develop 'within child' learning difficulties as a result of this. A lack of 'self-talk' from a guiding adult may result in the learner having weak strategies for talking and reasoning its way through new tasks – skills that are sometimes referred to as 'metacognition'. This may also result in having a weak ability to recognise that they have control over their choices and actions, which could then result in poor learning behaviours (see, for example, Dockrell and McShane 1992; Westwood 2004). Similarly, if the learner does not have access to a range of experiences and to language linked to these, then it is likely that their understanding of ideas and concepts will be weaker than those of other learners who have had these opportunities. Therefore, these environmental difficulties become part of their neural profile over time and become further compounded as time passes.

Another reason why this might be the case is that learners from lower socio-economic backgrounds are more likely to be exposed to a range of disadvantages that can have a negative impact on learning. There are many disadvantages which can affect someone's ability to learn, for example:

- poor school attendance;
- difficulties at home;
- an unstimulating environment;
- a culture of low expectations inside and/or outside of school;
- poor teaching and a failure to accommodate a range of learning styles.

Factors such as these are often referred to as 'social factors' and can have a significant impact on the ability of a learner to learn well.

It is easy to see, therefore, how a background of deprivation, combined with additional disadvantages such as those outlined above, may well result in a degree of general learning difficulty. A learner in these circumstances is therefore much more likely to be considered to have a MLD even though they may not necessarily have been born with any kind of neural deficit or intellectual impairment.

While these factors might be considered as part of the 'nurture' aspect of learning, it is also important to note that socio-economic deprivation does bring with it an increased risk of some 'within child' difficulties – those which might be considered to be aligned more with 'nature'. For example, socio-economic deprivation brings with it an increased risk of 'organic' risk factors such as premature birth and foetal alcohol effects, which are also correlated with MLD (Greenspan 2006, p. 212).

In addition, parents who have learning difficulties themselves are likely to have reduced earning potential, which means they are more likely to be over-represented in lower socio-economic groups. Parents who have learning difficulties may also find it harder to develop some of the aspects of development in their children through typical approaches such as modelling, talking and interacting with them.

The fact that many learners with MLD come from lower socio-economic backgrounds may have contributed to the fact that there appears to be a much weaker parental lobby in relation to learners with MLD than there has been for other SEN. Often professionals and parents might be keener to turn towards a well-known diagnosis such as 'dyslexia' when a child is presenting with difficulties in literacy and other core skills, than to consider whether these difficulties are indicative of a general cognitive weakness. While one reason for this might be a lack of awareness of MLD and of learning difficulties in general, it could also be argued that this reflects the 'stigma' that has been attached to learning difficulty over time. At this point it is useful, therefore, to briefly explore the social history of learning difficulty, particularly since this history impacts so significantly on current thinking in the field of SEN and disability.

Political and historical perspectives

While in schools we tend to refer to learning difficulties as a special educational need, it is important to note that MLD is also considered to be a disability. The Equality Act (2010) defines a disability as a 'physical or mental impairment which has a long-term and substantial adverse effect on their ability to carry out normal day-to-day activities' and defines long-term as 'a year or more'. The field of disability studies offers crucial perspectives on the experience of people with learning difficulties and that is why this point is significant to us in thinking about how we support learners with MLD.

Most significantly, there are strong historical and contextual factors at play here which we cannot ignore if we want to have insight in this area. Throughout history, people with disabilities have too commonly been accorded an inferior life experience compared to their peers. In many cases, they have variously been denied access to work, education, social life, housing and jobs; have suffered inferior legal and human rights; have been denied equal choice and opportunity for decision-making about their lives; have had their physical freedoms limited by society's failure to make physical spaces accessible; have had little public representation; and have experienced fewer opportunities for economic participation.

This has resulted in the labelling of people with impairments and learning difficulties, and their 'separation' from mainstream society into specialist establishments such as schools, care homes, institutions and hospitals. In many cases this has resulted in very limited life chances and lack of autonomy for individuals.

This approach is often referred to as the 'medical model', and has been seen by many as the dominant and traditional approach to learning difficulties and disability. (Indeed, it is worth noting as an aside that some commentators suggest that this perspective on people with disability is largely the result of the dominant ideology of the reliance on individual labour power under capitalism since the Industrial Revolution.)

The medical (or individual) model suggests that the problems experienced by people with learning disabilities and difficulties are the expected and unavoidable result of their own deficiencies. This model locates the problem of impairments within individuals, and it perceives any resulting disability as stemming from the functional limitations of the impairment itself (Oliver 1990). This is a model in which:

- A person's difficulties are diagnosed, in much the same way that an illness might be.
- A suitable diagnosis or 'label' is given, one which might be seen to highlight the difference between this person and a 'normal' person.
- Expert professionals decide whether any treatment or intervention is appropriate.
- The person is then dispensed this treatment in an attempt to improve or solve the difficulties they have. (In terms of education, some would argue that this is still evident when we recommend separate schools or 'special classes' or interventions where learners are taken to learn away from the rest of their peers.)

It is easy to see why this approach is so problematic, not least because it implies that the person with the learning difficulties is not 'normal' and is therefore somehow inherently different or more commonly inferior to others who don't have the same disability. It suggests that they need to be 'treated' alongside other people who have similar difficulties. It also leads to the assumption that the individual's difficulties need to be addressed and resolved as much as possible before they can even be considered for full inclusion in the mainstream.

It is also worth noting that many have argued that the representation of disabled people in the media (and, in particular, in charity advertising) has reinforced this perspective – often people with disabilities are presented either as survivors or victims of tragedy, or as objects of pity. With this comes the feeling that they are a burden; they have to be given different dispensations and allowances have to be made. There is a view that they do not bring anything of equal quality or value to the rest of us and we cannot learn from them. This is such a sad and naive view, as some of our biggest opportunities to learn come from those who require us to think creatively and adapt our approaches and ways of thinking.

Language matters

Much of the terminology that has been used to describe disability over time reflects society's negative attitudes towards people who have disabilities. In fact many of these labels imply that the problem lies within that person – that they have some kind of fault, a failing, a deficit in them which needs to be 'treated' or corrected.

Language is not 'just words' – it is in fact our most powerful means of conveying the thoughts, feelings and attitudes of people and of society. The labels which are attached to people have an impact on their views of themselves, their sense of status and dignity, how they're treated and the opportunities that are made available to them.

In our own schools, many of us will have heard learners with MLD referred to with terms such as 'remedial' and 'slow', terms which now sound particularly derogatory and offensive in tone. Over time, people have tended to become more aware of the connotations of such terms and, also, these words have taken on an increasingly negative tone, one which some would argue reflects society's continuing attitudes towards people with learning difficulties. Nevertheless, over time, words and phrases are reviewed and discarded when they are felt to have taken on negative connotations or when they no longer reflect current thinking.

Norwich and Kelly (2005) identify a number of terms which have been used to describe people with learning difficulties over time: 'mental deficiency, mentally defective, feeble-minded, mentally retarded, the backward child and the slow-learning child'. All these terms indicate that the person is somehow not a complete or functional human.

The language used to describe SEN and disability has frequently changed in response to shifting perspectives and attitudes. Nevertheless, phrases such as 'global delay', 'special needs', 'needy', 'weak' and 'low achieving' are still sometimes used interchangeably by staff in schools. Some of these terms are likely to sit uncomfortably with learners, their families and the staff who work with them. In order for us as advocates and supporters to effectively shape the respectful use of language and terminology in our schools, it is vital that we are aware of how the current terminology came about.

The term 'Moderate Learning Difficulties' was brought into common use by the 1978 Warnock Report. This report attempted to move away from a 'remedial' approach in which the learner was given a fixed label – such as ESN or Educationally Subnormal – towards a model which focused on identifying and describing what the child needs in order to make progress (see, for example, Norwich 2004; Warnock 1978).

This distinction may sound subtle, but is actually quite critical in terms of whether people with learning difficulties are seen as being fundamentally different from others. 'Moderate Learning Difficulties' specifically describes a level of difficulty with learning, which is less judgemental of the actual person than earlier phrases given the fact that many of us have some difficulties with learning at some time or other. Therefore, this change of language marks a shift from a perspective which locates the difficulties as a deficiency within the person, towards a model which acknowledges that, as learners, many of us need different styles of teaching or support in order to make progress with our learning.

As a result of this shift, much of the language of education for learners with MLD since 1978 has referred to learning and support needs in order to continue to avoid the negative associations that have tended to become attached to categories or labels. However, by trying not to label and pigeonhole learners who find acquiring information and knowledge hard, we are now in a situation where there is a lack of clarity about who it is we are actually trying to support.

It is vital in our work with learners that we ensure that the language used by staff and by learners themselves is respectful towards those with learning difficulties and disability in general. As supporters and advocates of learners with special educational needs, this is a challenge that we should not shy away from, and it is worth considering how we might address (or pre-empt) situations in which derogatory or offensive language is used to describe learners or their difficulties.

One key aspect of this is to consider how to respectfully challenge people who we encounter using derogatory language in schools – in many cases this can be as simple as saying, 'I wanted to make you aware that we don't use the term XX any longer because it is considered by lots of people to be offensive. Usually we would use the term XX instead'.

It can also be very valuable to set up training for learners and for staff on the Equality Act (2010), including ways in which this can be translated into our day-to-day practice. Many schools have chosen to involve learners themselves in running training and assemblies for staff and peers around issues of disability, diversity and terminology in general. Often these are extremely powerful because our learners can be incredibly honest about what they think and feel. In addition, this allows them to be central to work which involves them, their needs and views, and how they wish to be referred to and treated in school.

For the purposes of this book, we view any learner who is not making appropriate and expected progress to be someone who would benefit from adaptations to teaching described in this book. Put simply, a learner with a Moderate Learning Difficulty is one who has some difficulty learning and therefore needs to be given support to address the barriers they face. It does not matter why they find learning hard, but it is important to find out from them what can be done to make learning easier.

Issues of voice, power and agency

The dominance of the medical model over time has resulted in people with learning difficulties having less decision-making power than their peers. Often, decisions have been taken out of their hands and made by people who are seen as having superior knowledge – medical professionals, social workers, teachers, family members – often anyone except the person that these decisions involve. In many cases, therefore, people with disabilities have been denied a voice about such key issues as where they live, how they will spend their free time, what work they will do, what their education will look like and where it will take place. Many would argue that this amounts to a denial of human rights and this is one key aspect of the medical model which activists have campaigned to change.

In recent years, however, there has been a shift away from the medical model, as people with disabilities and their supporters have demanded equal rights. This has led to the emergence of a more equitable and person-centred approach, one which has the voice of the individual at its heart, and which emphasises the fact that people should not be defined by their impairments. This is often referred to as the social model. The social model recognises that society's attitudes towards those with disabilities are discriminatory and unequal and offers a clear and persuasive alternative to the medical model.

The social model tends to emphasise the fact that:

- People's own views and opinions must be central in any decision-making about their lives. In schools, for example, this might include decisions about what is most helpful with their learning, and what kind of support they find useful.
- Every person is of inherent and unfaltering value, just as they are. Individuals are not and should not be defined by any impairments or difficulties they may have.
- All people should be welcomed and included in mainstream activities, and adaptations should be made where necessary so that this can happen. People with disabilities should not feel compelled to take part in 'separate' or 'specialist' activities.
- Organisations and society as a whole must make necessary adaptations in order to be inclusive and to ensure equality of access. It is the failure to do this which 'disables' people, rather than the nature of their impairments and difficulties.

For those of us working in mainstream schools, therefore, the social model offers us both a framework for a more just and egalitarian way of approaching our work with learners who have special educational needs, and a valuable description of our end destination or goal as inclusive practitioners.

Issues for consideration:

From medical model to social model

How do your school's current practices reinforce the attitudes of the medical model? How might they be changed to reflect the shift towards the social model?

Medical model	Social model	Questions to ask
A person's difficulties are diagnosed (in the same way that an illness might be).	The individual is given the opportunity to express what they find difficult, what they find easy, what their goals and ambitions are, and what they do and don't enjoy. They are not defined by what they find difficult.	How often do we describe learners by the 'labels' they have been given? How often do we ask learners their views? How much do we involve their families? What status and importance do we give to this rich information – is it central to the planning for the learner?
The individual's difficulties are given a suitable 'label', one which might be seen to highlight the fact that the person is different from others.	Every person is of inherent and unchangeable value, just as they are. Individuals are not defined or described by any impairments or difficulties they may have.	In our organisation, how often do we hear words relating to SEN and disability used in a negative way? Do we make sure that, when we present positive role models and examples to our learners, we include people who have disabilities and SEN? Do we refer to learners as individuals with unique interests, strengths and difficulties, or do we tend to give prominence to their 'diagnosis' when talking about or with them?

Medical model	Social model	Questions to ask
Expert professionals decide whether any treatment (or intervention) is appropriate.	The learner's own views and opinions are central – they are asked what help and support they find most useful.	How often do we ask learners what they find most helpful? How much time do we put aside for 'quality' conversations with our learners? Do we adapt provision and support in response to their views? How often do we hold meetings about learners, or reviews of their progress, to which they are not invited?
The person is then 'treated' in an attempt to improve or solve the difficulties they have.	All people are welcomed and included in 'mainstream' activities, and adaptations are made where necessary so that this can happen. People with disabilities should not feel compelled to take part in 'separate' or 'specialist' activities.	How often do we teach learners with disabilities in 'special classes' or interventions? How do they feel about that? (How often do we ask their view?) Where classes are streamed or set, how do learners who are in the 'bottom sets' feel about that, and why? When they are in school, how much time does a learner with MLD spend, each week, away from their peers? How often is a learner paired with their TA rather than a peer during 'pair work' in class?

Figure 1.1 Medical to social model

Chapter 2

What do the learners think – and why should we listen?

Practical strategies for person-centred planning

It has often been the case in schools that learners have been considered to be the recipients of education. Decisions about what is learnt, how and where it is learnt have most often been made by teachers and other adults who have commonly been deemed to 'know best' about what learners need. Children and learners (and, indeed, parents) have rarely had a say in this, or had the opportunity to give feedback.

The passivity and low levels of personal agency within this approach have much in common with the medical model of disability which was outlined earlier. With this in mind, it is easy to see how learners with learning difficulties have been at least doubly disadvantaged by the way they have been dealt with by schools; not only are they pupils, and therefore inferior to teachers and other adults, but they are also learning disabled, and therefore often have even less opportunity to make their own decisions and choices.

As mentioned earlier there has been a growing critique of this approach, and a shift away from it. This can be seen in many cases as the result of campaigns by pressure groups and organisations to demand equal rights for all groups in society.

This pressure has resulted in human rights legislation such as the Equality Act (2010) which rightly emphasises the importance of equality and of personal voice for all people, in all settings, regardless of characteristics such as age, gender, marital status, sexual orientation, race and religion, among others. This has led to a growing awareness of the importance of ensuring that people's views are at the very least taken into account when decisions are made about their lives.

The SEND Code of Practice (2014) reflects this shift in thinking. It places great emphasis on enabling learners to have power over the decisions made regarding them. Unless it can be demonstrated that a learner is unable to make decisions for him or herself because they lack the capacity to understand the consequences of their decision, learners and their parents have the right to make choices. Indeed, the very first principle that underpins the guidance is that there must be regard to 'the views, wishes and feelings of the child or learner, and the child's parents'. The second principle reiterates this commitment to person-centred approaches by stating the need to have regard to 'the importance of the child or young person, and the child's parents, participating as fully as possible in decisions, and being provided with the information and support necessary to enable participation in those decisions'. Statutory guidance requires, therefore, that the voice of the learner is more than ever a central aspect of our work in the field of SEND.

There are many other reasons, though, why it is so crucial that we take time to find out what our learners think – and this includes all learners, not just those with MLD. Most importantly perhaps is the fact that our learners themselves are the only ones who are present in all aspects of their daily lives; nobody else has this 'inside knowledge' of what school and home life is like for them. If we ignore this rich source of information then we are missing out on a great opportunity to see what is working well and what needs attention. Indeed, it seems strange that we might ever imagine making judgements on these things without asking the learners themselves.

It is also important for learners to see themselves as active participants in the decision-making process. The status and importance that we give to their views is key: it gives a clear message as to how much we value their opinions, experiences, beliefs and preferences. It affects their self-esteem for better or worse. It gives them a clear taste of how much autonomy and power they can expect to have as adults – and allows them to practise expressing their views and making choices.

One good example of the importance of the learner's voice is in the area of target setting. If teachers and parents were to meet and set a learner's targets based on what we think they need to do, without consulting with them, it is highly unlikely that they will be sufficiently motivated to commit to and to achieve the targets – after all, these would be OUR targets rather than theirs. By contrast, a learner who has been involved in setting their own targets is much more likely to have their end goal in sight – they are more likely to have personal meaning, to be remembered and not forgotten, and therefore to be worked towards and committed to. This is discussed in greater detail below.

Positive cultures for listening

A good deal of work has been carried out in recent years in schools and colleges on ways to capture the voice of the learner and to make sure that planning and reviewing takes place in a person-centred way. Usually this is as part of the review process, as this is a means of ensuring that the learner's views are able to feed into clear and agreed actions.

Below are some pointers to consider when planning how best to gather learners' views in your setting.

It is vital that learners are provided with a regular opportunity to give honest feedback about their learning and experience of school, and to have these views listened to and acted upon where appropriate. Schools will need to think not only about how they can create a culture where this is welcomed, but also to consider their own systems and processes for ensuring that there is consistency and that learners are able to give a honest, broad and detailed view about their learning experience.

Learners can be part of student forums outlining what works and does not work for them. Learners can be given opportunities to identify what works in their lessons; this could be done for all learners and form a class charter about what they will do and what their teacher will do to help their learning.

Systemically, there are many ways in which this feedback can be captured for individual learners. A few of the most popular are detailed below:

- The learner takes part in a 'learning conversation' as part of a SEN Review or an Annual Review meeting.
- The learner takes part in a 'learning conversation' in advance of a review meeting, and their views are then shared – either by them, or by a supportive peer, family member or staff member, at their review meeting.
- The learner completes a questionnaire in advance of the review meeting.
- A questionnaire is sent home for the learner to complete with their parents or carers in advance of the review meeting.

Whichever of these systems is used, the most important thing is that time and space is given for quality feedback and listening to the learner's views. Therefore it is critical to plan to ensure a high-quality conversation.

The quality learning conversation

When deciding how you will capture a learner's views, it is really vital that you make sure that the conditions are right for them to be able to express what they really feel, without adults' opinions and perspectives having an undue influence.

Work with learners around their wishes and feelings needs to be carried out with an adult they trust – ideally they would be allowed to nominate the adult who they would like to do this work with.

It is also really important that consideration is given to questions of power and hierarchy. For example, it can feel very difficult for a learner to critique their support to the TA who provides that support. So time must be given to ensuring that the best possible opportunities are created for enabling the learner to have their say; sometimes this will mean that the conversation needs to be carried out with somebody who is not the learner's key worker and this will need to be decided on a case-by-case basis.

In some settings the feedback of learners can feel quite threatening at times and staff can be thrown onto the defensive, particularly when the feedback is negative. It is important therefore that all staff involved are clear about the expectations for such conversations with learners, and that they are professionally primed to be able to accept criticism without taking it personally. It is also important that, when questioning and prompting, they don't inadvertently 'steer' the learner towards expressing their own views.

This can also be true of conversations which are carried out with the parent or carer at home – as in the model of sending home a questionnaire before a review, for example. In the vast majority of cases, parents will of course be sensitive to the views of their child if they help them to complete the questionnaire – but there will also be occasions when the questionnaire reflects the parents' views more strongly than those of their child. Providing a parents' questionnaire may help with also ensuring that parents feel 'heard', but in any case it is certainly worth considering all of these factors when choosing which system to adopt.

There are times when a learner won't be in the right frame of mind for a reflective discussion and so some flexibility is also needed about when this should happen. If they are tired, or hungry, or have just had a difficult lesson and are feeling upset or angry, this may result in their responses not reflecting what they typically feel.

Liaison with parents

The SEND Code of Practice (2014) is clear about the need for parents to be involved in the assessment, planning and intervention of the needs of their children. This can be seen as a very positive development – after all, parents are a rich source of first-hand knowledge about their children. They are likely to have the clearest and most accurate idea about their children's strengths, difficulties, preferences and what support is likely to work for them.

For some parents, their involvement might be relatively straightforward. For example, it may simply involve speaking with them regularly about their child's progress and discussing with them what interventions could be implemented if appropriate. For other parents, maybe those who have English as an Additional Language, or those with disabilities themselves, more work will need to be done to enable them to fully participate in the discussions around what should happen for their child. This work can take various forms, including:

- a facilitator/advocate explaining to the parent in jargon-free English or their first language what is going on, why and what can happen next;
- a key professional being identified in the school to be the sole point of contact for the parent to discuss any issues concerning their child;
- parent forums where more systemic issues can be raised and resolved;
- parent drop-in sessions, where they can raise issues in more informal settings;
- teachers and staff visiting the family at home and having conversations with them on more neutral ground – this is especially important if school has been an issue for them;
- feedback being adapted to accommodate the learning needs of the parent, i.e. if they have reading difficulties, making the text accessible with pictures and simplified English can reduce barriers and increase their sense of voice.

It is important when working with parents that we do not just pay lip service to listening to them, but actively respond to their views, concerns and wishes. It may be that at times their wishes and desired outcomes are unfeasible, in which case the evidence and rationale needs to be shared with them, rather than parents feeling that something that they are entitled to is being withheld from them. Involving parents, listening to them and keeping them informed is key to moving things forward with their child.

Prompts for the learning conversation

Prompts can be a useful way of ensuring that the information gathered is as focused and relevant as possible.

The following pages include some prompts and frameworks which might usefully be used as the basis for a learning conversation with a learner. These can be completed together and used as a 'starting point' for gathering and recording the learner's views.

My learning conversation

Name _____ Date _____

This conversation was held with _____

I feel that my strengths are…

After school and college, I plan to…

Three things that are going well at school are...

Three things that are not going well at school are...

If I could change three things, they would be…

In lessons, I find it most useful when…

I would like adults working with me to be aware that…

I find these things most difficult…

My learning conversation

Name _____ Date _____

This conversation was held with _____

How are things going right now?		
What's going really well?	What's going okay?	What's going badly?

Why are these things going well?		What would help with this?

What do you want to happen in the future?		
This year?	When you leave here?	When you are an adult?

My learning conversation

Name _____ Date _____

This conversation was held with _____

👍	These are the best things about school for me:	
👎	These are the things I'm not happy about:	
	These are the things I would like to change:	
	These are my wishes for the future:	
	I would also like to say that:	

My learning conversation

Name _____ Date _____

This conversation was held with _____

_____

All these ideas are to do with your learning and your future.

Talk them through with the adult and use them to prepare a 'mind map' of your views.

- Your subjects and lessons in school
- Your friendships
- Your hobbies in and out of school
- Your relationships with teachers
- Your relationships with people in your classes
- Your support in school
- Break and lunchtimes
- How well you feel respected
- How well you feel listened to
- Clubs and activities
- Your future plans

My views

Figure 2.1 My learning conversation

Visual representations

Some learners find it more useful to be able to share their views in a visual way and this too can be a rich source of information. For example, on a simple level, learners might be encouraged to express their ideas through drawings, pictures or photos (perhaps with captions).

Alternatively, materials can be prepared which scaffold responses through visual means: this might include, for example, a sheet with a sunny scene on one side and a rainy scene on the other. The learner has to decide which aspects of their school life they would allocate to each side of the sheet and note down why (or an adult can scribe this). Similarly a sheet could include smiley and sad faces, or pictures of self now and in the future to denote ambitions and plans, or empty bowls which can be filled up with emotion pictures and words.

These formats are ideal for individual learning conversations, but would need to be adapted for conversations that take place within an actual review meeting.

At the review meeting

One popular approach for person-centred planning at a learner's review meeting involves flipchart sheets displayed on the walls. A key focus of the meeting is that the learner as well as perhaps their family and adults working with them have the opportunity to note down their observations about the learner's educational experience. Prompt questions in this situation might include:

- What we most like and admire about...
- What's important to...?
- What does .... need in order to succeed?
- What's working well?
- What's not working?
- Our hopes and plans for ....'s future.

One crucial aspect of prompt questions such as these are that they should be positively framed and focused on the learner's wishes and feelings. When carried out sensitively, we have found this kind of review to have the potential to be a real celebration of the learner, their character, strengths and achievements, as well as an effective action plan around their aspirations for the future.

Much has been written about person-centred planning as well as ways to capture the voice of the learner and it is certainly worth staff in schools taking some time to think about how best to do this. The most important factors are that the medium chosen meets the learner's needs and they feel able to be honest and open about what is important to them. It is this sensitivity, combined with an ongoing process of honest reflection about how we are capturing these views, which will allow our SEN review processes to have the voice of the learner at their heart.

Future planning

One essential aspect of person-centred planning is ensuring quality opportunities for exploring future goals, aims and outcomes with learners. Ideally, this process should be ongoing and revisited regularly. Some learners will have little idea of what options exist for them beyond the world of school, and therefore discussions about future aspirations and outcomes can be highly valuable and worthy of attention in terms of time and resource.

The resources that follow are intended to provide staff with seven short sessions worth of 'prompts' which can be used to stimulate discussion and thought around future possibilities, with a view to exploring and clarifying a learner's long-term aspirations and goals. These goals can, in turn, be used to provide focus for the target-setting process, which is explored in further detail later in this book.

Envisaging the future

From aspiration to target

> These prompts and strategies can be used in mentoring sessions to help learners to explore and clarify their future goals and aspirations.

Session 1

Ask the learner to imagine life when they are 25.

- What is the best life they can imagine having? What would be the best job, car, house, place to live, friends, hobbies that they can imagine?
- What is the worst life they could imagine having? What would be the worst job, car, house, place to live, friends, hobbies that they can imagine?

Make notes about their best life and keep these safe, ready to revisit next time.

Session 2

In the next session, ask the learner to imagine that they are 25. Ask them to answer the following questions as their 25-year-old self:

- What's your name?
- How old are you?
- What is your job now? How much do you earn?
- Did you have to get qualifications at school to do this job?
- How did you manage to do well at school?
- How did you manage to stay out of trouble when so many others got into trouble? Did other students ever try to get you into trouble and how did you handle this?
- Did teachers ever get on your nerves?
- How did you manage not to get sent out of lessons?
- What did you do when you found the work difficult?

Session 3

The next area for discussion is: 'What can help me or hold me back from achieving my dream?'

- Which people will help you to achieve the life you want?
- What skills will help you to achieve the life you want?
- What personal qualities (honesty, kindness etc.) will help you to achieve the life you want?
- What might get in the way?

Session 4

Ask the learner to list people they admire for what they can do. Discuss: What have these people done and achieved that you admire?

Ask the question, 'What is an aspiration?' and draw out the point that an aspiration is a hope for the future that you want but don't yet have. They can start work on achieving it right now though. Ask what goals and aspirations they have achieved in their life so far.

Discuss with your learner the fact that aspirations are achieved one step at a time, and usually with commitment and hard work! The future life that they want will be the result of achieving a number of small goals or targets along the way.

Ask them to think about a goal or target they have achieved. Use an example of a skill from your life to prompt talk. Ask them to think through these questions:

- Could you do it straightaway?
- How did you get to be able to do it?
- Did you learn it all at once or a little bit at a time?
- Was it ever hard?
- Did you ever feel that you didn't want to practise?
- Did you ever feel that you wouldn't be able to do it?
- Did you ever want to give up?
- How did it feel when you could do it, when you achieved what you set out to do?

Session 5

Discuss with the learner what people need to do to achieve their future plans:

- They have a vision – they know where they want to be.
- They take one step at a time.
- They believe they can do it.
- They know that what they do is up to them – they don't make excuses.
- They tell themselves they can do it.
- They keep the long-term plan in mind.
- They keep going, even when it's hard.
- They practise, practise and then practise some more.
- They know they will fail sometimes but they keep going anyway.

Session 6

The next step is to help the learner to break down the big picture into smaller targets or goals. What are the little steps to achieve their preferred future? Discuss together and make notes on these questions:

- What is your target for one year after you've left school?
- What is your target for the day you leave school?
- What is your target for the next year?
- What is your target for the next three months?
- What is your target for next week (one thing I am going to do to help me to…)?

Then ask the learner to consider what would have to happen before they could achieve that target. The key learning point is that targets become more specific and precise as they become more immediate. Finally, ask the learner to write their own specific target for the next two weeks.

Session 7

This session is about thinking about the next week only, and reiterating the links between short-term planning and long-term goals and aspirations. Review the learner's target which was set last time, and their progress in achieving this. Ask whether they intend to stick with this target, or amend/adapt it for the coming week.

When they have settled on a target for the forthcoming week, discuss how they will overcome any obstacles that they face. Some points to consider together are:

- why this target would be a good thing to achieve;
- why I'm not doing it: my reasons and excuses;
- what will be hard about taking the first step towards my target;
- what I can do to overcome the obstacles.

Figure 2.2 Envisaging the future – from aspiration to target

Practical strategies for academic target-setting

Thus far we have focused on the most effective way of setting person-centred targets, primarily as a 'stepping stone' to a learner achieving their long-term goals and aspirations. It is also important here to consider the role and functions of targets in schools, as these are sometimes at odds with the person-centred model and are often set by teachers and school leaders, rather than being generated by the learner themselves. Schools vary a great deal in the way that they use targets, and indeed even in what they mean by 'student targets'.

In some cases, 'student targets' refer to target grades or levels. In recent years, this has often referred to the grade, level or age-related expectation which the learner is expected to achieve by the end of the year or the key stage, and often reflect progress which is in line with national expectations.

Sometimes, more challenging 'aspirational' targets are set. These reflect an expectation that the learner should be expected to make greater than average progress – for example, they might be expected to make three full levels of progress during each key stage. Sometimes aspirational targets are set because a cohort of learners might be working at such low levels on entry that they are supported to try to 'catch up' as much as possible with age-related expectations during their time in secondary school. Often this is accompanied by additional interventions in subjects and core skills. This is most often the case in schools where attainment on entry is low, and where GCSE results will also be very low unless learners are helped to make faster or 'accelerated' progress.

Often learners will be made aware of their data target and will be expected to be able to articulate this, to talk about what grade they are aiming for, and hopefully how they will achieve this.

One purpose of grade and level-based target-setting is to ensure that there are high expectations for progress for all learners. Ideally, they should be a point of focus for teachers and support staff, and a motivator for learners. However, there are particular sensitivities when we are using data targets for learners with MLD, many of whom will have made less progress over time than their peers, and who may therefore struggle to achieve progress in line with that of their peers. It is vital therefore that data targets are also set with this in mind, in order to ensure that these are achievable targets and that they are likely to motivate rather than demotivate the learner.

Target grades and levels are also usually supported by written 'small step' targets. These provide a clear summary of what skills or knowledge the learner is aiming to achieve next, in order to make learning progress. Schools have a range of systems for setting short-term outcomes – sometimes these are set by or with subject teachers, sometimes by or with the tutor, and sometimes learners with SEN have separate targets set as part of the review, IEP or PSP process.

The combination of data targets and written targets, when used effectively, can be extremely powerful in supporting good learning progress. They have the potential for ensuring that the learner, their parents or carers and adults working with them all know what they are aiming for, and what they need to do next to get there. This is equally true for learners who have MLD, who will benefit from knowing exactly what they need to do next, as do all learners. It is for these reasons that target-setting and reviews are considered to be best practice at all levels of school improvement.

It is vital, however, that targets are written with the learner, rather than for them. When targets are written on behalf of learners, they are less effective because the learner is unlikely either to recall what they are or keep them in mind, and in addition are less likely to feel motivated towards them. The target-setting conversation should be collaborative in nature, and should involve school staff, the learner and their parents or carers. Ideally subject teachers should also have an input, whether through being present in person, or where this isn't possible, by providing written suggestions as to possible next steps for the learner. The agreed targets should relate and contribute to the learner's long-term goals and aspirations (referred to in the Code of Practice for SEND as 'outcomes') as well as to the learner's data targets.

It is likely that the term 'short-term outcomes' will increasingly be used in place of 'targets' as the new Code of Practice becomes embedded in schools. For ease of use, however, the sheets that follow refer to targets. These can be adapted in schools where short-term outcomes becomes the terminology of choice over time.

Steps to academic target-setting

When adults set the targets there is a 10 per cent improvement in behaviour. When learners set the targets for themselves, there is a 40 per cent improvement in behaviour. Learners need to be committed to and know what they are aiming to accomplish.

Learners cannot be successful if they are not aware of their targets.

Positive outcomes are more likely when targets are carefully chosen and agreed. This increases self-esteem; energises learners to persist with challenging tasks; reduces failure-avoiding behaviour; and increases optimism and hope about future challenges.

Negotiating effective academic targets with learners

Always discuss targets in positives
What do you want specifically? What are you aiming to achieve? Why?
When, where, with whom do you want it?

Allow the learner to have ownership of the target
Achieving success cannot be dependent on the actions of another person or situation. It must be within the control of the person who wants the target to happen. Key questions to ask are: Who wants this to happen? What resources do we have to make it happen? Do you need any help to achieve this target?
What will help you to achieve it?

Help them to visualise and imagine success
Be as specific as possible. Discuss with the learner: How will you know when you have achieved this target? What will you see, hear and feel? What will success look like, sound like and feel like?

Put it into context
Discuss with the learner: How will this target help you? What will it allow you to do, once you have achieved it? What difference will it make? When will you use this skill?

Check that it's a worthwhile target
Discuss with the learner: What impact will achieving this target have on your future plans, and the rest of your life? What will happen if you don't achieve this target?

Plan for shared monitoring and review
Discuss with the learner: How long do you need to achieve this target? When shall we get together to check how it's going? When are we aiming to have achieved this?

Figure 2.3 Target setting

Many staff working in schools will be familiar with the concept of 'SMART' targets, and we feel that they deserve a particular mention here. The effective use of SMART targets can lead to much clearer targets, and much more easily identifiable results. These are targets which are:

S – specific; rather than general.
M – measurable; easy to see whether it has been achieved or not.
A – achievable; it is realistic for the learner to aim for this goal.
R – relevant; it is well-considered and relates to the learner's needs.
T– time-bound; a clear length of time is set out for the target to be achieved.

For learners who have MLD, this provides a very valuable framework for ensuring that the targets that are set with them are understandable and that successes are easy to identify and can be celebrated.

Here is how it works:

Target: I will improve my writing.

We can establish whether this is a valuable or relevant target by looking at the learner's current attainment and strengths. This particular learner, for example, could have a developing sense of what a sentence is but be very sporadic in their use of capital letters at the beginning of new sentences. However, this target is far too general for anyone to know exactly what success will look like, what the specific aspect of their writing they need to develop is, or how we will know when it's been achieved. So it needs to be more specific:

Target: I will improve my writing by starting new sentences with a capital letter.

Already this is much clearer. However, it would still be difficult to see when this has been achieved. Do we mean every sentence or just some new sentences? If some, then how many – two or three? What if they achieve this in one piece of work and then forget? So let's make it measurable:

Target: I will improve my writing by starting at least nine out of ten new sentences with a capital letter.

This is now both measurable and (depending on the learner in question) is also more likely to be achievable than if we expect that they will achieve this target every single time.

We have already established that this is a relevant target for the learner in question. So let's think about timescales – when will we review whether this target has been achieved? We know that it needs to be long enough for the skill to be practised and secured, but short enough to maintain focus and pace and be able to recognise the learner's success in a timely way. So let's make it time-bound:

> Target: In the next six school weeks, I will improve my writing by starting at least nine out of ten new sentences with a capital letter.

This is now a much clearer target and one which is much easier to understand and measure. It might also be worth thinking about how exactly the learner will demonstrate that they have met their target – one valuable way of giving them ownership is to put the onus on them to share their evidence, for example at their next review meeting. So the target might then become:

> Target: In the next six school weeks, I will improve my writing by starting at least nine out of ten new sentences with a capital letter. I will show that I have done this by bringing my books from English, COPE and RE to my next review meeting.

This target is now very clear, measurable, and easy to use to assess progress and to identify success. One key feature of effective target-setting is that the targets need to be kept current – all too often they are only revisited when review time comes around and by that point everyone concerned has forgotten what they were. There are a number of ways in which the focus can be maintained in the meantime:

- Targets are recorded in exercise books and referred to in lessons.
- Targets are recorded in homework diaries or student planners.
- Parents have a written record of the targets so they can remind the learner when they are going through their homework, for example.
- All teachers and support staff are aware of the learner's targets and give reminders of these.
- The learner has a laminated key ring or bookmark with their targets on.
- Written and verbal feedback in class refers to the learner's targets.
- Usually a learner will have a maximum of three written targets at any one time, as more than this is likely to feel unachievable and will also be increasingly difficult for the learner and teacher to keep in mind.

The most inclusive practice in this area is when all learners, rather than just those with SEN, have an opportunity for collaborative target-setting. In recent years, targets for learners with SEN have often been set through the IEP process, but increasingly this approach is falling out of favour. There are a number of reasons for this. For example, the IEP process has been found in many schools to be overly bureaucratic, to take responsibility for the learning and progress of learners with SEN away from the class or subject teacher, and to suggest that learners with SEN need a different 'system' to their peers if their difficulties are to be remediated.

Therefore an increasing number of schools are seeking to integrate target-setting for learners with SEN into the whole-school systems, and to record any additional support or provision on a provision map. Since the introduction of the most recent SEND Code of Practice (2014), some schools are choosing to introduce alternative, person-centred systems of communicating key information, such as 'pupil passports' or 'individual profiles'.

Whichever model is used, it is still important to ensure that there is a means whereby learners with SEN can access quality target-setting which accurately identifies the 'next steps' for their own progress, and which signposts the way towards their longer-term goals and aspirations. This clarity means that staff in school and the learner's parents can also support the learner in achieving their goals, thereby enabling the best chance of success.

Chapter 3

Wouldn't it be better if they had some more time in Learning Support?

Exploring whole-school approaches to Special Education and inclusion

Many of us will have been asked by a colleague, at some point, whether a learner can be taken out of a lesson to complete their work elsewhere. Sometimes this may be because their behaviour is challenging in the classroom, they are finding the lesson work too difficult, they are felt to be 'too far behind' their peers, or are unlikely to achieve a grade G/C/Level 5 (delete as appropriate!). Sometimes we are asked to withdraw them for a lesson or part of a lesson, and sometimes for a longer period or even permanently. Sometimes colleagues will ask whether a learner who has SEN might not be better served in a special school.

As adults who teach and support learners who have learning difficulties, it is important that we are aware of the implications of where we choose to teach learners who have special educational needs. This is not to say that there is a clear and universal 'right or wrong' answer; every child and situation is clearly different and the wishes of the learner and their family must be paramount. Rather, it is vital that we consider honestly and carefully the reasons why we are thinking about withdrawing a learner from a subject or lesson – is it to help the learner, or is it to make life easier for us as staff?

When we make these decisions, we need to be mindful of where people with special educational needs and disabilities have traditionally been educated. Historically, people who were seen as 'different' were often removed from public view and placed in mental institutions, special schools and care homes. Many felt that such people were unteachable and therefore could not make a meaningful contribution to society. Often they were denied the opportunity to be educated alongside their peers, a denial which many in the disability rights movement might identify as an enforced segregation, similar in many ways to the racial segregation that was evident, for example, in American schools for much of the twentieth century.

For learners with special educational needs and disabilities in the UK, there was a significant shift in educational policy following the Warnock Report on *Special Educational Needs* in 1978. This report led to greater opportunities and greater inclusion for learners with special educational needs. Since 1978, successive governments have introduced and reinforced policies of educational inclusion, which have in turn led to the closure of many special schools. This has led to an increasing number of learners with learning disabilities and difficulties being educated in mainstream schools. This is reflected by national policy which now supports the vast majority of adults with learning difficulties and disabilities to live in the community.

In spite of this shift towards social and educational inclusion, there continues to be a continuum of perspectives on whether learners with additional needs should always be included within the mainstream school. Many feel that it is beneficial for everyone that all learners are educated alongside their peers – regardless of need or difficulty. The opposing view is that learners with additional needs require a specialist curriculum that can only be provided in specialist settings.

The reality is that there is no single, simple answer which is true for all. What is right for one learner may not be the most appropriate or suitable option for another. The social model of disability puts the choice of the individual at its heart, and there are learners who, supported by their families, feel strongly that special school is right for them. It would not be in the spirit of the person-centred, social model to deny that this is the case, nor to expect that all learners with SEN be taught in mainstream settings.

There are certainly many arguments in favour of educational integration and inclusion. Gross (2002) for example, provides several compelling arguments why educational inclusion is desirable:

- It is a point of human rights that everyone should have equal access to membership of the same group.
- There has been 'consistent failure to find evidence that the assumed benefits of education within special schools can be demonstrated' (p. 233).
- There are very clear benefits for learners of going into school with learners from their neighbourhood.

It has also been argued that learners with additional needs – as is true of all learners – benefit from having positive role models around them to inspire them, teach them and encourage them. One of the biggest drawbacks to specialist education can be the lack of strong learners as role models, meaning that learners do not see what they should be aiming for, what learning looks and sounds like, and how they can achieve it. One of the most significant ways that learners acquire behaviours and information is by referring to and copying 'models' around them. If these models are experiencing the same difficulties as them then they may be less likely to make good progress.

Social integration and the opportunity to form positive peer relationships is often given as a reason in favour of mainstream education for learners with special educational needs. Kelly and Norwich (2004) have, for example, found that learners who attend specialist provision are more likely to be bullied by learners at mainstream schools than are learners with additional needs who attend mainstream schools.

Other educationalists provide equally powerful arguments in favour of special schools. For example, there is a strong argument that the curriculum in special schools provides an invaluable combination of academic and vocational skills, often combined with supervised work experience. Phelps and Hanley-Maxwell (1997) argue that this is a crucial means of ensuring that learners with special educational needs obtain jobs and therefore achieve inclusion in their local community as adults.

What is crucial for us as staff, though, is that we are fully respectful of a family and learner's choice about where they are to be educated, and that we commit fully to making this as successful as possible.

What is also clear is that the teaching principles needed for learners with MLD are beneficial to all learners, regardless of need. It is also clear that it is right and proper for teachers to develop their teaching skills to cater for a range of learners, rather than just those who actively can, and want, to learn. All of our classes contain a range of learners, and as teachers and support staff we need to cater for all their needs.

Regardless of where a child is educated, be it in a mainstream or specialist setting, everyone involved in teaching and learning needs to do just that: 'teach and learn'. Inclusion can benefit us, too. As teachers and support staff we learn from our students. We learn what works, what engages them, what may be too hard and what may be too easy. In return we teach them our knowledge and skills. How can we convince our learners that learning is worthwhile and rewarding if we are not prepared to engage in it ourselves?

Teachers of learners with additional needs have the opportunity to develop the skills necessary to adapt their teaching to cater for a range of needs. They increase the diversity of their teaching, which is more engaging for all learners, reduces the effort needed to teach, and also improves behaviour.

Inclusive education can be beneficial to all learners, not just those who have special educational needs. For the learners we teach, the world we live in means that they will encounter people with learning difficulties and additional needs in their lifetime, in their community. It therefore makes sense that we actively teach all learners to work cooperatively together, rather than create barriers that will need to be overcome later on in life. Acceptance, diversity, difference and individuality are all important elements of learning and these aspects help us to differentiate one from another.

So does it benefit anyone else? The answer is yes. Learners learn most effectively when they have to teach others, so by showing learners how they have solved a problem, or explaining it to someone using more simplified language, they are reinforcing their learning and developing their neural connections. The process of breaking information down and reconstructing it requires a deeper understanding of the information and concepts involved. Learners who are exposed to a more diverse school population tend to be more accepting of others with differences when they are older and they are better able to adapt to different ways of thinking and working.

For the community, seeing learners being accepted by their peers, encourages adults to be more open and accepting of others with difficulties and differences. It encourages the community 'to look after its own' and this encourages a sense of cohesion and solidarity within the community, making it stronger and more resilient in the long run. By fostering a sense of belonging within schools, people are less likely to become isolated and therefore will be better able to contribute to the community they live in. In this way, everyone has a vested interest in supporting each other and everyone has a part to play.

As a whole school, all staff should feel empowered and confident in teaching learners with additional needs. Those staff who are apprehensive about having a learner who struggles to read the text, or a learner who is still unsure of number bonds to ten, are justified in recognising that they will need to change the way they teach a bit; they may need to teach the same topic a number of times and this can be daunting. However, it is also remarkably rewarding to see the learner who could not read stand in front of the class and read aloud from the textbook because you have pre-taught them the key vocabulary and they have accessed additional individual support to improve their overall reading skills. It is not easy, and cannot be achieved by one teacher alone, or one specialist unit. But with a truly inclusive school, all learners can show they are both teachers and learners.

By isolating learners, the myth that there is a specific way to teach 'these learners' is reinforced and everyone becomes slightly unsure of how to interact with, work with, and befriend those who are different. In these circumstances we all lose out on learning opportunities.

Including learners with MLD

So, what can teachers actually do to teach learners who find it hard to learn? How can they be actively included, rather than just present in the classroom to satisfy external expectations? In the final chapter, we explore concrete examples of resources and strategies that can be used to support inclusion within the classroom. However, there are four key aspects that are fundamental to the inclusion of all learners in your classroom.

1 Firstly, you need to have a clear idea of what the learners you are teaching are able to do. Assessments need to have a purpose, rather than just to inform data capture, and they should inform your understanding of the learners you are teaching. If you don't know what a child is able to do, or more importantly how they learn best, then you need to find out. Speak with your colleagues, the SENCo, outside professionals, the parents and their previous teachers to gather this data.

2 Once you have this information, it should be clear where the gaps in knowledge and learning are. This information can be combined with information that the SENCo should have about the learners' ability and areas of difficulty, for example SAT scores from primary school, NC levels, CAT scores if appropriate, as well as reading and spelling ages, to give a clearer indication of areas that may be difficult for them.

3 With this information, you can then identify topics that are going to be harder or teaching methods that will be less successful.

For example, if a learner has a low reading age, giving them a lot of written material is going to be difficult for them to read, understand and use appropriately, so you could use a video clip or pictures instead. The way to differentiate material is dependent on the topic being taught and the needs of the learner, but using a range of modes and presenting information a number of times to enable ample opportunities for learning, will maximise the likelihood of learners learning the information being taught.

4 Finally, it is important to review the progress being made to ensure that the teaching strategies are effective. Talk to the learner, ask them how they found the

lesson, is there anything that could be done to make the lesson easier for them? Do this after teaching them using different methods and compare results. While it sounds very labour intensive, if you find out that they learn well from role play but can't recall anything from listening to information, you can use this information to plan your lessons and not waste time trying to engage them in tasks which they find too challenging.

Teaching – do we need to use a different approach?

When we take the time to really reflect on learning, what becomes clear is that a lot of what goes on in lessons is task-orientated – we too often tend to focus on 'getting work done' or sometimes even 'filling up the lesson' rather than really planning for deep and relevant learning.

So what changes need to occur to enable teachers to focus on deep learning rather than task-specific information?

- If learners come into classes without prior learning and knowledge in a specific area, they can be given additional support to develop these skills before being expected to apply them in more complex ways. This is crucial because if learners have not had an opportunity to acquire a piece of information or skill, then they are not going to be able to become fluent with it, generalise it to other situations or adapt the learning to novel or new contexts. Therefore it is vital that learners are aware of the skills that they need to draw upon for the task at hand and that opportunities for learning these skills is provided if necessary.
- If learners have successfully acquired the necessary information, they should be able to recount what they have been taught in their own words and they should be able to provide a brief explanation as to why it was taught. It should make enough sense to them that they are able to assimilate the information (merge it) with previously learnt knowledge and understand how it fits in to a bigger picture.
- If learners are only ever taught how to recount information but not to assimilate it with previously learnt knowledge, then they will find it hard to store, recall and use the information in different settings and contexts, called 'generalisation and adaptation'. The skills necessary for higher grades at GCSE require the use of skills such as explaining, evaluating, describing and comparing. In order to develop these skills, learners need to know that the knowledge they learn does not exist in isolation, but in conjunction with other facts and skills. An analogy for this might be a painter who does not learn that she can blend new colours from the primary colours she has in front of her, and who is therefore only able to produce a fraction of the paintings that she would otherwise have been able to paint.
- Similarly, by using learning hierarchies such as Bloom's Taxonomy to support our planning as teachers and support staff, we are able to ensure appropriate challenges for learners at all stages. This means that we are less likely to 'build on sand' as we progress through the curriculum, but instead build a solid foundation. It also provides invaluable opportunities for differentiation, and thus for inclusive teaching and learning, within individual lessons.

Teachers sometimes express a desire to learn the 'secrets' of teaching learners with MLD. This view assumes that learners with MLD need to access a specialist model of teaching, which holds the key to unlocking their potential. In addition, there is often a feeling that the current approach of inclusion is somehow letting these learners down because the appropriate method of teaching is being withheld.

Norwich and Jones (2014) have acknowledged that a number of the pedagogical approaches and strategies that are effective with learners with MLD derive from a unique differences approach. This is one which focuses on the needs that are distinct for individuals as well as the needs that are common for all. Therefore, in contrast to the general differences position (which holds that, in addition to focusing on needs that are distinct for individuals and common to all, there is also a focus on common attributes associated with the definition of a category, i.e. how are all learners with MLD different from other students), learners with MLD require the same teaching approach as learners without these difficulties. Adjustments need to be made for pace, mode of presentation and response, and exposure of information. But these adjustments are true of all learners – no-one will learn the skills necessary after a rapid, single exposure to a theory, problem or concept.

By looking at what individual differences learners with MLD have, rather than looking at how this category of learners are alike, we are able to tailor appropriate intervention as opposed to assuming that they will all benefit in the same way to the same general interventions and approach.

Learning support units: the secure base

While most learners with special educational needs benefit from being educated within mainstream classrooms and schools, there are some times when they need to access specific interventions to develop the skills that they have difficulty acquiring, such as reading, remembering facts, numerical operations, vocabulary etc. These interventions can often be best offered within small learning environments, where distractions are reduced, staff access is high and the skills and information taught are specific. In addition, the evidence base indicates that interventions which are short, time bound and conducted on a daily basis are the most effective.

When offered in this way, these interventions can facilitate and promote access to a safe and secure base where learners who have difficulty learning can go when they need to reduce the stress of learning or they wish to have some 'down time'. We often forget that learning is very tiring for all of us, but even more so when it requires more thinking, attention and processing capacity than would normally be attributed to the task. By offering learners with additional needs a safe place to go, they can start to regulate their interactions with their peers and their information intake. The secure base also reminds all learners that they are valued, wanted and safe at school. This is vital for learners if they are to trust adults enough to learn from them.

However, in order for it to be considered a safe base, rather than to be seen as their classroom or unit or school, they need to be supported for the majority of the time in a mainstream learning environment. If this does not happen, staff and learners will gradually forget they are part of the school and isolation and segregation is likely.

Effective use of teaching assistants

The use of teaching assistants (TA) is now commonplace in mainstream schools, and there is a growing body of research which aims to capture their impact and the value they add to learners' progress.

While teachers find the additional adults in a classroom helpful and reassuring, the evidence suggests that in order for them to impact on progress they need to be skilled and included within the planning of the lesson being delivered. Where this doesn't happen, research suggests that the support of a TA can have a neutral or even a negative impact on learning progress (for example, Blatchford et al. 2007).

This fact can seem surprising when we consider the invaluable support and assistance that many of us see TAs provide in schools, and is contrary to what we might assume. It would seem much more likely that young people in receipt of additional help would make more progress, not less.

There are a number of reasons why the research suggests that TA support can have a negative or neutral impact on learning progress, and it is worth giving these some consideration. Let's consider for a moment the experience of James, a Year 8 learner with MLD who is supported by his TA Mr Oatley in 12 lessons a week.

James enjoys being supported by his TA Mr Oatley – he is always kind, supportive and there to help. Mr Oatley wants James to complete all of his work to the highest standard – even at times when James himself is not that bothered. (Sometimes James is tired, and there are some lessons he likes less than others.)

James relies on Mr Oatley a lot to help him in lessons. In fact, he prefers it when Mr Oatley explains things to him – so much so that he doesn't always listen to his teacher, to be honest. Mr Oatley also helps him when the work is too hard, by giving him sentence openers and key words, and then sitting next to him while he writes. If he is feeling tired, then sometimes Mr Oatley will scribe for him.

A lot of the work is too hard for James, because some of the teachers don't really understand his ability or what differentiation might be needed – they tend to leave that side of things to Mr Oatley and then he makes things easier for James. Most of James' teachers are really grateful that he has support because James doesn't usually want to talk to them very much or answer any of their questions. If he doesn't understand something, he will usually ask Mr Oatley rather than the teacher.

It is easy to see from this example that the support James has, while highly valued by him and his teachers, is making him less of an engaged learner and more of a passive dependent. There are many issues with this model of support, but particular points to consider might be that:

■ Mr Oatley is focused on James getting work done, rather than learning anything.

- Teachers are not differentiating for James, or really engaging with him very much at all, because he has such close TA support.
- James is, in effect, getting most of his 'teaching' from his TA, rather than from the subject-specialist teacher.
- James does not need to bother listening to the teacher because Mr Oatley will explain it to him separately, meaning that all the information he gets is 'second-hand'.

It is easy to see how such a model is likely to have a negative impact on a learner's progress over time, and yet all-too-often it is this model which we rely upon to include our learners with MLD, even when it is these leaners who are most in need of direct, high-quality teaching by subject-specialist staff.

This leads to some important points about 'help' and 'rescue'. We have all worked with learners who frustrate us, who don't grasp what we are trying to teach them and who appear to lack the motivation needed to engage with the task. For these learners, it is so tempting just to do the work for them and move on. However, if this is what we teach them, that in fact they are not able to learn this, then they will start to learn that they are not capable, cannot learn and so should not try. In the long run, they become the hardest learners to engage and teach and their behaviour often deteriorates.

With these learners, if you invest in teaching them the skills needed, they will learn that they are worth investing in, can acquire the knowledge and will invest in their own learning, thus reducing the burden on you and your team.

All learners need to feel successful on their own, especially if they are to develop their independence and self-confidence. If someone is taught that they can only do something with someone aiding them, they will learn to expect this and feel anxious and frightened when presented with a task that they have to do on their own, either by design or default if their TA is off one day.

Everyone is able to do some tasks on their own and there should be times when learners are encouraged to engage in these tasks. When TAs are used, they should be used to extend the work that someone is able to produce on their own – not to compensate for someone's inability to do a task independently. It is vital, then, that tasks and activities are appropriately tailored to the learners' needs so that they can attempt them with as much independence as possible.

What does a learner need to know before they can do a task on their own?

They need to know:

- what the 'problem' is – they know what it is that they have been asked to do;
- where they need to start – they know what the first thing they need to do is;
- how to create a plan for completing the task – what the finished product should look like;
- what they are actually 'making' or 'solving' – what the final product will consist of;
- how to evaluate their performance – they know what was good about what they have done and what areas they can do better in next time.

Before learners can apply their previous knowledge to a situation they have to know what it is that they have been asked to do, what previous information will help them figure out where they need to start, have an idea of the stages they will need to work through, what the end product should look like (a story, poem, maths sum, model, drawing, a specific behaviour etc.) and how they can improve on this next time.

If a learner is struggling to do a task on their own, it is worth considering these areas before proceeding. This can help staff to 'break down' where exactly the area of difficulty is, and to adjust or support as appropriate so that they can then proceed independently.

Support towards independence: a guide for TAs

Teaching assistants can extend a learner's thinking, in collaboration with the teacher, by:

■ Asking questions, particularly open-ended questions such as:
  - How can you...?
  - What did you...?
  - Where might you...?
■ Providing prompt sheets – giving cues as to what the learner needs to include, or the process they need to work through.
■ Providing clear objectives and instructions. Be explicit about what is required, using visual cues if needed to reinforce key messages. Be clear about what it is they need to do in order to be successful and what the point of their learning is.
■ Making sure the meaning of the task is clear. Be explicit about why they are being taught this skill/knowledge – how it will help them and why they need to know it.
■ Varying the level of challenge – ensuring the task is neither too easy nor too hard. If the task is too hard, they will not be able to access it on their own, and so they will always need support to do it. If the task is too easy, they may see that they are not competent and so will give up. There has to be a sense of accomplishment when they are successful. If tasks that are being provided by the class teacher are not pitched appropriately, then TAs should make the teacher aware of that – if they don't know, they can't address it!
■ Varying the speed of presentation and working at their speed:
  - If they are fast workers, match their pace and try to slow them down so that they think carefully about what they are doing (particularly for learners who struggle to get things correct and rush through the learning tasks).
  - If they are slow workers, gradually increase the expectations of what they need to do in a set time. For learners who focus on accuracy over speed, use timers to limit the time spent on a task and make sure they have enough time to process the information given to them.
■ Providing structured feedback – give feedback as they work through a task, highlighting the positives about their approach, such as:
  - 'Well done on starting there...'
  - 'That is a good use of the word...'
  - 'I am impressed you remembered to...'
■ Using a variety of modes to present information and obtain responses – ensure that the task is presented in an accessible way. Try to include a range from:
  - visual
  - auditory
  - verbal
  - kinaesthetic.

- Developing their memory and linking new information into information they have previously been taught – use familiar materials and encourage them to think about times when they have done something similar to assist their memory and recall. What information have they already learnt that can help them? Repeating instructions and key pieces of information. Using memory games.
- Developing their logic and strategic thinking – encourage them to think hypothetically about how they can solve the task:
    - What do they need to do?
    - What evidence do they have to go on?
    - What do they need to collect?
    - What can they infer and deduce from what is already available?
- Encouraging the use of strategies – get them to create a plan for how they can solve the problem/task. Get them to list the steps they need to take to answer the question.
- Ensuring the learning environment and task are emotionally safe:
    - Reward learners for great effort and great thinking (rather than praising when they get it right and encouraging them when they get it wrong!)
    - Remind them it is okay to make mistakes.
    - Give them breaks when you can chat about things other than the work that needs to be done.
    - Show you are interested in them.
    - Create a shared goal for what needs to develop and see how much progress has been made on a daily/lesson-by-lesson/week-by-week basis.
    - Teach them calming strategies if they become easily distressed or anxious.
- Prioritising information so that you are focusing the learner's attention on the most important elements:
    - highlight
    - underline
    - point towards the key words or key pieces of information.
- Encouraging the use of reflective evaluations:
    - Check over work.
    - Evaluate progress.
    - Rate their performance.
    - Discuss – what, if anything, has been different to their last piece or to their expectations?
    - What has been different?
    - How are they going to proceed through the next task (this will highlight any issues or misunderstandings)?
- Using concrete resources to facilitate understanding of time and the task (for example timers and visual cue cards).

Figure 3.1 Support towards independence: a guide for TAs

Withdrawal from the classroom

There are two schools of thought about where the most effective TA support can be provided. Do you try to support learners in the classroom and hope they can focus with the background noise and potential distraction, or do you withdraw them to a quiet space and teach them the key messages away from the rest of the class? The answer is highly dependent on the child and what they need to be taught.

Most learners with MLD are likely to enjoy learning with their peer group as much as possible. Some do not like being withdrawn at all as they feel it makes them feel 'special' and 'different'. On the other hand, there are others who find that having someone with them in lessons makes them 'stand out' as different from their peers – a situation which can sometimes be addressed by more flexible TA use in the classroom, supporting a group of learners, for example, or circulating around the classroom. There are also learners who prefer the quiet and opportunity to focus that withdrawal from the classroom can provide.

Personal preference varies greatly in this regard. Each learner is different and the nature of support will depend on what it is they need to learn, what they find most useful and what specific difficulties they face. Most interventions that are based on withdrawal from the classroom are most effective when done for a short period each day, and when done for a set number of weeks (i.e. they are not withdrawn on a permanent basis), so that the learner can see that the intervention is time limited and therefore an 'added extra' not a replacement.

With support in the classroom, having adults who can support small groups as well as the target learner can also reinforce the message that all learners need support at times, and it may even be that the TA can work with the most able, while the teacher works with those who require the most input.

Targeted interventions for specific skills

While learners with moderate learning difficulties can be included within the learning activities of the mainstream class, there are times when learners may require specific interventions to develop specific skills that will assist them within the classroom. For example, interventions might usefully address specific areas of difficulty in:

- literacy – sometimes discretely addressing reading, writing, comprehension, vocabulary, spelling and phonic skills, but more often a combination of these;
- handwriting;
- numeracy;
- concentration;
- memory;
- self-care;
- life skills;
- social skills and interactions;
- emotional and behavioural regulation;
- speech and/or language skills.

Before you begin an intervention, it is vital that you think carefully about what skills you are targeting, how you will help learners to improve these skills, and which type of need your intervention is aimed at.

Most interventions take place for a limited period of time and as frequently as possible within that. Usually, for example, there is more impact to be made by working with a learner for one hour a day for 20 days than for seeing them 20 times across the whole school year. This is because they are likely to need frequent practice and rehearsal of target skills to get them to the point of 'automaticity' – being able to do those things without thinking.

Good intervention also then includes monitoring and follow-up afterwards to ensure that the learners are maintaining and applying the target skills.

It is important that these interventions are conducted in conjunction with the learning of the classroom, so that they reinforce the messages and information being taught, thus increasing the likelihood that the learning will be perceived as relevant and the connections in the brain will be activated.

Figure 3.2 can be used as a 'frontsheet' or 'topsheet' record for each intervention you are running, in order to identify clearly from the outset the aims and timescales of the piece of work.

Intervention topsheet

Name of intervention	
Staff member	
Start and end date	
Number of learners	
Frequency of intervention	
Duration of intervention and total number of sessions	

Target skills:

Skill	Activities to practise target skill

Post-intervention monitoring and maintenance:

Methods of post-intervention monitoring and skills maintenance:

Figure 3.2   Intervention topsheet

Ensuring impact

It may sound an obvious point, but it is important to make sure that the interventions we run with learners are likely to make a positive difference or *impact*. We want to know that, following an intervention, they have improved their skills or confidence in at least one area. After all, there is little point in running an intervention that makes no positive difference to a young person's learning, or, even worse, that results in negative impact!

It is for this reason that schools are increasingly looking very closely at the *evidence base* of various interventions before they choose which ones to run – this means the body of information that has been gathered about what difference an intervention makes, and to which skills.

There are various ways in which you might gather this information:

- For interventions which are available to purchase commercially, the makers will usually be able to signpost you towards their body of impact data.
- There are a growing of number of reports and surveys which attempt to summarise the impact of a number of interventions, so that schools can more easily compare interventions and the difference they make. The following reports and publications are popular examples of this and provide a valuable starting point for staff looking to investigate further the matter of impact:
  - *What works for pupils with literacy difficulties? The effectiveness of intervention schemes* by Greg Brooks;
  - *The Sutton Trust – EEF Teaching and Learning Toolkit.*
- Specialist advisory agencies such as Speech and Language Services, Educational Psychology, Behaviour Improvement Teams, and so on.
- Professional journals.
- Colleagues in other schools and settings.

It is important to look critically at any impact data on any given intervention and to consider whether the results are likely to be transferable into your setting. For example, you might usefully ask:

- Where and when was the impact data gathered?
- What was the sample size – how many children were involved?
- Were they of the same age and did they have similar difficulties to the young people you are working with?
- How frequently did they access the intervention and for how long?
- Were the results sustained after the intervention ended?

We would argue that all schools should regularly review the interventions they use. Very often we decide which interventions to run on the basis of what the school already has in place and running, and it can be very tempting to stick with these for the sake of simplicity. However, it is vital that we keep this under review because the research base and the number of interventions available is always growing, and so we can often benefit from reviewing what's available as time goes on.

Equally as important is the need to evaluate the impact of our own interventions, in our own settings. This means we can be sure that they are actually having a positive impact on outcomes for learners in our schools, and if this is not the case, then we can investigate why this might be and respond appropriately.

There are a number of reasons why evaluation of impact is such a valuable exercise:

- to know we are helping our learners to achieve positive outcomes;
- to help us understand 'what works' for learners with specific needs and difficulties in our own settings;
- to know exactly which skills are improved on which intervention – meaning we can match learner to intervention even more effectively in future;
- for our own professional confidence – meaning that we know, can prove and can confidently argue that our work brings positive benefits to our learners;
- to help us be accountable to our school leadership teams, to parents, staff, students and inspectors;
- to help us show 'value for money' in the way we spend our SEN funding and pupil premium;
- to help us to argue persuasively for additional resources when we need them.

The most common and simplest way of evaluating the impact of interventions is to gather a set of core data before the intervention begins, to repeat the exercise afterwards, and to compare the two sets of data. This data might include a range of measures, including:

- the learner's own view of their confidence and competence in the specific target skills (see sample self-report sheets on the following pages);
- staff judgement of their confidence and competence in the specific target skills;
- attainment data such as National Curriculum levels, age-related expectations, reading and spelling ages etc.;
- attendance, punctuality and behaviour data.

The pages that follow feature a number of examples of the way in which impact data might be measured for a range of interventions. These can easily be adapted to include the specific skills that your intervention is targeting, and therefore to ascertain what impact the intervention has had, by individual learner and by group.

The three learner self-report sheets provide a way of quantifying how the learner feels about their own skills and confidence, before and after an intervention. This data can then be compared, alongside other measures such as National Curriculum levels and so on, in order to build up a picture of the intervention's impact, firstly by individual learner and then across the cohort by averaging the scores. The sample intervention evaluation sheet in Figure 3.7 provides a framework for how this might be done.

In addition to gathering this broad range of measurable data, we believe that it is also worth asking learners some very simple questions about whether they found an intervention useful, and recording their responses. This not only allows us to maintain our focus on person-centred practice, but also provides a useful triangulation of the data comparison outlined above. Key quotations from learners' responses can then be typed at the bottom of the intervention evaluation sheet to illustrate the learners' own views of the intervention and flag up key issues and successes.

How's it going right now?

Name: _____   Date: _____

Year: _____   House: _____

	I feel good about myself.	I know how to stay safe.	I think I'm a good friend.	I know how to stay calm.	I am kind.	I am on time.	I can calmly explain what I want.	I am happy in school.	I feel listened to.	I am looking forward to the future.	I work hard.	I eat well.
Very true												
Not at all true												

Figure 3.3 Learner self-report for social, emotional and mental health interventions

How's it going right now?

Name: _____ Date: _____

Year: _____ House: _____

Very true										
Not at all true										
I feel good about myself.	I feel confident adding numbers up to 10.	I feel confident adding numbers up to 20.	I feel confident adding numbers up to 50.	I feel confident with describing shapes.	I feel confident with measuring.	I feel confident subtracting or taking away numbers.	I can do most sums in my head.	I am confident with fractions.	I can tell the time.	I know my times tables.

Figure 3.4 Learner self-report for numeracy interventions

How's it going right now?

Name: _____

Year: _____

Date: _____

House: _____

	I feel good about myself.	I feel confident with my reading.	I feel confident with my writing.	I feel confident with my spelling.	I feel confident with my speaking in English.	I feel confident that I can understand what people are saying.	I feel confident that I can think of the word I want to say.
Very true							
Not at all true							

Figure 3.5 Learner self-report for literacy and language interventions

Prompt questions for learner voice on intervention impact

(To be completed at the end of the intervention)

Did you find this extra help useful?

Why or why not?

What have you learnt or improved?

What can we do to make it even better next time?

Figure 3.6 Prompt questions for learner voice

Name of learner:	House and Year:	Data prior to intervention:		Data after intervention:		Difference:	
Jeremiah Sharkey	Phoenix, Year 8	How's it going right now?		How's it going right now?		How's it going right now?	
		I feel great about myself	2	I feel great about myself	3	I feel great about myself	+1
		I feel confident with my reading	2	I feel confident with my reading	2	I feel confident with my reading	0
		I feel confident with my writing	2	I feel confident with my writing	3	I feel confident with my writing	+1
		I feel confident with my spelling	4	I feel confident with my spelling	2	I feel confident with my spelling	-2
		I feel confident with my speaking in English	3	I feel confident with my speaking in English	3	I feel confident with my speaking in English	+2
		I feel confident that I can understand what people are saying	1	I feel confident that I can understand what people are saying	5	I feel confident that I can understand what people are saying	+3
		I feel confident that I can think of the word I want to say	1	I feel confident that I can think of the word I want to say	1	I feel confident that I can think of the word I want to say	0
		Attainment:		Attainment:		Attainment:	
		English NC or GCSE	2a	English NC or GCSE	1a	English NC or GCSE	-3
		Reading age – decoding	7:02 years	Reading age – decoding	7:08 years	Reading age – decoding	+ 6 months
		Reading age – comprehension	8:04 years	Reading age – comprehension	8:08 years	Reading age – comprehension	+ 4 months
		Engagement:		Engagement:		Engagement:	
		% Attendance:	78.2%	% Attendance:	81.2%	% Attendance:	+3%
		% Punctuality:	81%	% Punctuality:	83%	% Punctuality:	+2%
		Behaviour Score:	99	Behaviour Score:	189	Behaviour Score:	+90
		ATL English:	red	ATL English:	green	ATL English:	+2
		ATL Maths:	green	ATL Maths:	green	ATL Maths:	0
		ATL Science:	amber	ATL Science:	green	ATL Science:	+1

Name of learner:	House and Year:	Data prior to intervention:			Data after intervention:			Difference:		
Didier Hollaway	Pegasus, Year 9	How's it going right now?			How's it going right now?			How's it going right now?		
		I feel great about myself	2		I feel great about myself	3		I feel great about myself	+1	
		I feel confident with my reading	2		I feel confident with my reading	2		I feel confident with my reading	0	
		I feel confident with my writing	4		I feel confident with my writing	5		I feel confident with my writing	+1	
		I feel confident with my spelling	4		I feel confident with my spelling	2		I feel confident with my spelling	-2	
		I feel confident with my speaking in English	3		I feel confident with my speaking in English	3		I feel confident with my speaking in English	0	
		I feel confident that I can understand what people are saying	1		I feel confident that I can understand what people are saying	4		I feel confident that I can understand what people are saying	+3	
		I feel confident that I can think of the word I want to say	1		I feel confident that I can think of the word I want to say	1		I feel confident that I can think of the word I want to say	0	
		Attainment:			Attainment:			Attainment:		
		English NC or GCSE	3a		English NC or GCSE	2a		English NC or GCSE	-3	
		Reading age – decoding	7:02 years		Reading age – decoding	7:08 years		Reading age – decoding	+ 6 months	
		Reading age – comprehension	7:01 years		Reading age – comprehension	7:05 years		Reading age – comprehension	+ 4 months	
		Engagement:			Engagement:			Engagement:		
		% Attendance:	88.2%		% Attendance:	91.3%		% Attendance:	+3.1%	
		% Punctuality:	79.2%		% Punctuality:	81.2%		% Punctuality:	+2%	
		Behaviour Score:	99		Behaviour Score:	189		Behaviour Score:	+90	
		ATL English:	red		ATL English:	green		ATL English:	+2	
		ATL Maths:	green		ATL Maths:	green		ATL Maths:	0	
		ATL Science:	amber		ATL Science:	green		ATL Science:	+1	

Name of learner:	House and Year:	Data prior to intervention:	Data after intervention:		Difference:	
					How's it going right now?	
					I feel great about myself	+1
					I feel confident with my reading	0
					I feel confident with my writing	+1
					I feel confident with my spelling	-2
					I feel confident with my speaking in English	+1
					I feel confident that I can understand what people are saying	+3
					I feel confident that I can think of the word I want to say	0
					Attainment:	
					English NC or GCSE	-3
					Reading age – decoding	+ 6 months
					Reading age – comprehension	+ 4 months
					Engagement:	
					% Attendance:	+3.05%
					% Punctuality:	+2%
					Behaviour Score:	+90
					ATL English:	+2
					ATL Maths:	0
					ATL Science:	+1

Average gains:

Learner comments:

'I am definitely more confident now. Before I used to hate reading out in class, but now it's not too bad.'

'One good thing was improving my spelling. One bad thing was being taken out of French.'

'I am much better at spelling now and my mum thinks so too; other people think so.'

'I would like more of this.'

Figure 3.7 Sample intervention evaluation sheet for literacy intervention

Chapter 4

How do we learn?

What is learning?

We often find ourselves having to clarify what is meant by learning. We generally, within an educational context, assume it to mean when people acquire the socially appropriate and desired knowledge that will enable them to be successful. We think of teaching as being something that happens in lessons; knowledge that has to be explicitly taught. However, learning in its base form is about developing an approach, skill or knowledge set which is actually based on experience, observation, direct guidance or a lack of response.

To make this a bit clearer, let's think for a moment about babies learning to crawl. They are rarely given specific guidance about what they have to do; instead they watch others moving around the room and mimic the mobility that they observe. This is in fact an important point to note. It highlights the fact that we all learn from things in our environment, some of which were not intended to be taught.

This fact is evident in much of what we do and see in our work. We have all seen learners who are aggressive because they have observed a parent who is violent. We have probably also all witnessed teachers who, without meaning to, give the message that only those who are bright are valued and given attention in the classroom.

Our non-verbal messages can be just as influential as the words we use; sometimes even more so. The first thing therefore is to be aware of the ethos that you create when you work with learners in school. Think for a moment about:

- Your view of what it is you are teaching or supporting. Do you encourage questions? Are you engaging? Do you model curiosity and interest? Do you show that errors are a useful and positive part of learning – or are you looking for the 'right answer' so you can move on? Are your sessions about 'doing work' or are they genuinely about the excitement of learning?
- Your attitude towards your learners. Do you take time to listen to them? Do you value their opinions? Do you genuinely want them to do well? Do you praise effort, kindness and commitment, or just academic success? Do you call them by name? Do you talk to them directly, or mainly via their TA?

The reason we ask these questions is because the right learning climate is vital if learners are to feel comfortable enough to learn. In fact, we often have the mistaken idea that learners with MLD are oblivious to what is going on and can't learn. The reality is that they are often very astute as to what is going on around them, especially what people think of them. Often they are able to learn very efficiently and may just need an adjusted pace or for information to be presented in a different way. Therefore, a positive, learning-focused and inclusive ethos in the classroom must be the starting point for outstanding learning and teaching.

Theoretical perspectives on learning for all

There is no single agreed model of what happens when we learn. Rather, there have been many educational, psychological, neurological and anthropological theorists who have presented a very broad range of models for learning.

We intend here to briefly outline the theories that have had the greatest influence on our collective understanding of child development and stages of learning.

Bloom's Taxonomy

Benjamin Bloom was an American Educational Psychologist who chaired a committee which produced a taxonomy of objectives for students. Bloom's Taxonomy provides a range of skills and tasks in order of challenge, meaning that mastery has to be achieved at the lower levels before a learner can progress to the higher levels.

Skills		Activity
Creating: can the student create new product or point of view?	highest level of challenge	assemble, construct, create, design, develop, formulate, write.
Evaluating: can the student justify a stand or decision?		appraise, argue, defend, judge, select, support, value, evaluate.
Analyzing: can the student distinguish between the different parts?		appraise, compare, contrast, criticize, differentiate, discriminate, distinguish, examine, experiment, question, test.
Applying: can the student use the information in a new way?		choose, demonstrate, dramatize, employ, illustrate, interpret, operate, schedule, sketch, solve, use, write.
Understanding: can the student explain ideas or concepts?		classify, describe, discuss, explain, identify, locate, recognize, report, select, translate, paraphrase.
Remembering: can the student recall or remember the information?	lowest level of challenge	define, duplicate, list, memorize, recall, repeat, reproduce state.

Figure 4.1 Bloom's Taxonomy

This taxonomy is still in wide use in education today. For staff who are working with learners who have MLD, it can be extremely useful as a means of differentiating and personalising learning within a topic or theme. In addition, it can also be used as a way of signposting progression within a theme.

Here is a brief illustration of how this might be used in practice. Let's imagine a mixed-ability lesson which is aiming to revise the plot and key themes of *Romeo and Juliet*.

- The first level of skill within this lesson might be at the stage of *remembering* – can learners recall the key events in the plot, and which characters were involved in them?
- The second level of skill might be *understanding* – can learners who are working at this stage explain why the events of each Act unfolded as they did?
- The next level of skill might be *applying* – can learners who are working at this stage illustrate the ways in which suspense is created as the events of the play unfold?
- The highest level of skill might be *analysing* – how does Shakespeare's use of language contribute to the dramatic tension at key turning points in the play?

Using Bloom's Taxonomy to structure the levels of challenge within this lesson allows for an inclusive and personalised lesson plan to emerge – all learners are focusing on the same content, but with differentiated skill sets and outcomes at different levels of challenge.

It is also worth considering Bloom's Taxonomy as a useful tool for 'unpicking' what has happened when a learner or a group of learners have failed to grasp key ideas and concepts within a lesson. There are times when it is worth tracking back to the earlier stages to ensure that they are able to recall or grasp the key facts before building up the level of challenge from there.

Haring et al. and the Learning Hierarchy

Norris Haring and his colleagues identified the different stages that a learner needs to go through in order to fully own, know and be able to 'use and apply' a new skill or piece of knowledge. They called this the *Learning Hierarchy*.

The Learning Hierarchy (Haring et al. 1978) has four stages: acquisition, fluency, generalisation and adaptation. According to this model, in order for any information to be fully embedded in our consciousness and to be used seamlessly, it needs to go through this process. This is true for young learners and adults alike. It is why, for example, when we go on training courses we often do not heed the advice and suggestions of those delivering the training, because being told it once does not mean we learn it. What differs between people is the length of time spent at any one stage, so some people need more opportunities to go over the different stages in order for something to be fully learnt. Therefore learners with MLD may not always need to be taught differently every time, but rather to have opportunities for **more** learning in the same way.

Using the Learning Hierarchy

Use this checklist in the classroom or in intervention to support high-quality learning.

Learning stage	Indicators from learners	Strategies to try	
Acquisition Outcome: The learner can perform the skill accurately with little adult support.	Is just beginning to learn skill Not yet able to perform learning task reliably or with high level of accuracy	Adult demonstrates target skill to learn – modelling approach needed Adult thinks aloud to show their approach, especially for skills that are not explicit, for example, 'Which picture would go first, well this one has… so must go after…' etc. Learner has models of correct performance to consult as needed (e.g. correctly completed maths problems on board) Learner gets quick feedback about correct performance Learner receives praise and encouragement for their effort	Beginning stages of learning and mastering something new.
Fluency Outcomes: The learner: a) has learned skill well enough to retain independently; b) has learned skill well enough to combine with other skills; c) is comparable with their peers in terms of both speed and accuracy of correct recall.	Gives accurate responses to learning task Performs learning task slowly and with uncertainty	Adult structures learning activities to give learners opportunity to participate Learner has regular opportunities to repeat the target skill and practise it alongside other skills Learner gets feedback on fluency and accuracy of their attempts Learner receives praise and encouragement for increased fluency	

Learning stage	Indicators from learners	Strategies to try
Generalisation Outcomes: The learner: a) uses the skill across settings, situations; b) does not confuse target skill with similar skills.	Is accurate and fluent in responding May fail to apply skill to new situations, settings May confuse target skill with similar skills (e.g. confusing '+' and 'x' number operation signs)	Adult structures academic tasks so that the learner can use the target skill regularly in tasks Learner receives encouragement, praise and rewards for using the skill in new settings and situations If learner confuses target skill with similar skill(s), they are given practice items that force him/her to correctly discriminate between similar skills Adults work in collaboration with parents to identify tasks that the learner can do outside of school to practise desired skills Learner gets opportunities to review and to practise target skill to ensure maintenance
Adaptation Outcome: The adaptation phase is continuous and has no exit criteria.	Is fluent and accurate in skill Applies skill in novel situations, settings without prompting	Adult helps learner to articulate the 'big ideas' or core element(s) of target skill that the learner can modify to face novel tasks, situations (e.g. fractions, ratios, and percentages link to the 'big idea' of the part in relation to the whole) The learner is given opportunities to practise the target skill with modest modifications in new situations and settings with encouragement, corrective feedback, praise and other rewards Learner is encouraged to set own goals for adapting skill to new and challenging situations Link times when used similar skills before and clarify if any of them are appropriate for this task

New learning is becoming increasingly secure.

Figure 4.2   Using the Learning Hierarchy

Piaget and the stages of child development

Jean Piaget was a Swiss psychologist who was active for much of the twentieth century.

He proposed that all learners move through four fixed stages, and progression on to the next stage is dependent on mastery of the current stage (Piaget 1959).

The four stages are:

- sensorimotor (birth – 2 years of age) – which is characterised by the fact that an infant's knowledge of the world is limited to his or her sensory perceptions and motor activities. As such their behaviours are limited to simple motor responses caused by sensory stimuli.
- preoperational (2 years – around 7 years of age) – which is characterised by the development of language and symbolic thought. This period is marked by centration, irrevisibility and egocentrism, meaning the child tends to see things as fixed and from their own point of view.
- concrete operational (about 7 – about 11 years of age) – which is characterised by the ability to apply mental operations to concrete events, such as addition and subtraction.
- formal operational (adolescence into adulthood) – which is characterised by the ability to think logically about abstract and theoretical concepts.

This means that, if learners have not had the opportunity to develop mastery of a phase, they are essentially 'stuck' until they can develop the necessary skills. This is the model which has been highly influential in our current educational system.

In Piaget's view, learners naturally learn from their environment and they are naturally curious about what is going on in the world around them. In this model, the teacher is far less influential in learning and development than the intrinsic cognitive capacity of the learner and their own desire to engage with the world.

Vygotsky and the Zone of Proximal Development

Lev Vygotsky was a Russian psychologist who theorised the way in which learners develop reasoning and cognitive function. He researched and wrote in the early part of the twentieth century.

According to Vygotsky (1978), learners' acquisition of new information is guided by, and also shapes, their cognitive development. There are some developmental processes which only become activated when they interact with adults or cooperate with peers within their environment. Those with more experience (adults and older learners) model and structure the learning experiences for younger learners (King and Saxton 2010); this is also known as scaffolding (Wood et al. 1976).

Vygotsky suggested that learning is optimal when people are presented with tasks that are too challenging for them to complete alone, but with guidance, help and support – when the task is scaffolded for them – they are able to complete it successfully. This level of challenge or difficulty is known as the *Zone of Proximal Development* and it is during the occasions that tasks are just too difficult to complete alone, but can be completed with guidance, that the best learning happens. He highlighted the fact that learning is a social experience, and that knowledge is a social construct.

Vygotsky reinforced the view that a person's learning is related to both their cognitive capacity as well as the learning environment within which they are taught. It highlights the fact that people have learning potential which is fluid rather than fixed, thereby illustrating the interactive nature of cognitive development. For us in our work in schools, this suggests that if we can provide the optimal learning environment, then there is huge potential for the individual to learn and develop in cognitive skill and function.

Vygotsky saw cognition not as a static state, but as something which is constantly evolving and responding to the context and environment that the person is in.

Feuerstein and Mediated Learning Experiences

Reuven Feuerstein was an Israeli psychologist and a student of Jean Piaget. He took on a number of Piaget's views. However, it was through his use of standardised materials and his own experiences of cognitive assessment that Feuerstein developed his own theories of cognitive modifiability and of mediated learning experiences (1983).

Feuerstein's theory of mediated learning experiences states that, rather than just providing direct learning experiences which learners respond to independently, as suggested by Piaget (1959), it is more beneficial for the teacher to intervene with the learning experience by making it more meaningful, engaging and related to past and future events. In this way, learning is actively shaped and moulded by adults. Therefore the teacher is key within this model of learning.

Feuerstein and Jensen (1980) define mediated learning experience as:

> that which takes place when an initiated human being ... interposes himself or herself between the organism and the stimuli impinging on it and mediates, transforms, reorders, organises, groups and frames the stimuli in the direction of some specifically intended goal and purpose.
> (Feuerstein and Jensen 1980, p. 409)

Feuerstein's theory of mediated learning brings together a number of Piagetian concepts of cognitive development, such as conservation, and the Vygotskian concept of the zone of proximal development (Deutsch 2010). It also incorporates and recognises the impact that genetic and environmental factors can have on learning.

According to this view, successful teaching is reliant on the learner identifying the meaningfulness of the information, being engaged in learning and developing links to information previously taught (Mentis et al. 2008). Therefore, it is an approach used by Educational Psychologists when assessing learners and can be used in order to inform specific teaching strategies which may be particularly beneficial to target learners who may require more individualised teaching plans. There are pointers to further reading on Feuerstein's work at the end of this book.

Neuropsychology and neuroscience – how the brain learns best

The human brain is made up of millions of cells which are connected together and form pathways and templates. These pathways learn through repeated exposure, so the more often we see something, touch it, taste it and feel it, the more active the connections in our brains are. This means that frequent, repetitive activities are more easily learned than novel and infrequent ones.

Over time, as our brain capacity increases and we are able to engage in higher-level thinking (such as comparing, contrasting, explaining and describing) we spend less time learning the basic skills and more energy on being efficient.

In addition, chemicals present in our brain affect what we pay attention to. Situations which are stressful and frightening will lead us to learn to avoid those features in the future. This is significant when we think about how we teach in lessons – putting a learner 'on the spot', for example, by choosing them to read aloud from a text or to answer a question that is too hard for them, is unlikely to lead to quality learning if it induces a state of terror in the learner in question.

We often cannot recall much about why we avoid such high-stress situations and what other factors were present at the time. In addition, this type of learning can be damaging to our brain development by gradually destroying the cells in our brain and stopping the development of more productive and efficient pathways.

In contrast, learning which is fun, positive and stress-free enhances our brain's growth and facilitates the development of beneficial and efficient neurological pathways.

In order to learn anything, we need dopamine to be released in the brain. Dopamine is the main chemical that creates synapses in the brain. Synapses are tiny gaps between the outsprouting of two nerve cells. The more nerve cells we have, the more connections we make and the better able we are to perform complex behaviours. Therefore, the more synapses we have, the more connections we have and the better able we are to learn.

Dopamine release is primarily under the control of the limbic system (see Figure 4.3) – also sometimes known as the social and emotional brain. Learning is the building up of connections between nerve cells to form templates which, once created, can be accessed more easily. Most significantly, perhaps, is the fact that this process is primarily directed and controlled by the emotional brain.

This is a fundamental point for several reasons:

1 If a learner has a good emotional connection with the person who is teaching them, they are more likely to learn.
2 If a learner has an emotional interest in the material, they are more likely to learn.

Stress is also very good at releasing dopamine. However, in contrast to positive learning, stress releases dopamine in a flood that covers nerve cells rather than being a precise action, in the same way that we may water delicate plants with a spray bottle, rather than a bucket. Chronic stress over weeks and months can theoretically lead to a loss of dopamine. Stressful situations such as not understanding what is expected, being punished or being in an uncontained environment can be detrimental to learning.

In addition, stress produces adrenaline and noradrenaline which drives memories into the unconscious part of our memory. This is why we can recall not liking something, or being a bit apprehensive about going to the dentist, but we are not quite sure why. Therefore, if we want to learn and be able to recall effectively, learning needs to be positive and unstressful – perhaps in quite marked contrast to the traditional model of the 'strict and scary' school.

Neomammalian brain – this is the part of your brain you can see on the outside and it envelops the other two parts of the brain. It contains the neocortex which enables us to plan for the needs of others as well as the self. We are able to turn our thoughts inwards and observe ourselves and our own mental life.

This is our metacognitive ability – the ability to think about thinking. This is the area that enables us to be aware of our learning. It is unable to affect the reptilian features of the brain, so if people are scared, angry or anxious then they won't be able to engage in higher-level thinking.

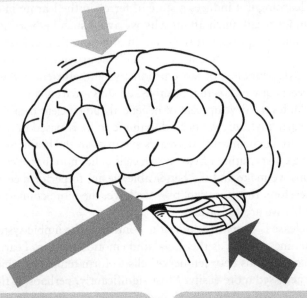

Limbic system/paleo mammalian brain – this is the emotional brain, which transformed our egocentric selves into social animals who nurtured their young and lived together in communities. This increased the number of nerve cells our brains had and so increased our ability for more complex behaviours, such as social interactions. However, it does not have the capacity to take over the reptilian brain, instead its function is to support our survival through nurturing and social behaviours.

Reptilian brain – a simple structure which is fairly poor at responding to novel situations. Its aim is to preserve its own existence with little concern for anything else. It has a set of relatively primitive structures that are vital for keeping us alive, e.g. keeping our heart beating. It also contains the amygdala which is concerned with our 'fight' or 'flight' sequences. Its desire for survival is what makes it egocentric, self-serving and appetite-driven, and it lacks a conscience.

Figure 4.3 The triune brain

Over time, different areas of our brain have adapted to different tasks, such as processing visual information or working out mathematical problems. However, most of our cognitive skills – attention, memory, language, perception, affective factors, logic and metacognition – have developed to utilise a number of different areas of the brain to enable greater efficiency. Our brain is very elastic and as such it is open to change, and so while damage to certain areas can be challenging for learners, we often find that other parts of their brain develop to compensate.

The most significant area of our brain, in terms of modern-day learning, is the frontal cortex (located within the neo-mammalian brain, at the front, see Figure 4.3). It is the part of the brain which is responsible for planning, inhibiting and selecting actions, controlling emotions and decision-making – all of the skills which we often ascribe to older and more cognitively able learners.

It is this part of the brain that we need to activate in all of our learners in order for them to be efficient and effective. We can do this by making them more aware of what we are teaching them, and by helping them to understand and to recognise how they learn best. One of the most common ways in which this is done in schools is through the method of metacognition – awareness of learning – which can be done through *Assessment for Learning*.

Assessment for learning

Assessment for learning has been adopted by the DfE as a model of teaching which encourages learners to be more active, aware of and involved in their own learning. Research has indicated that AFL strategies have the potential to lead to very significant accelerations in learning progress. The UK Assessment Reform Group (1999) identifies the five main principles of assessment for learning as:

1 the provision of effective feedback to students;
2 the active involvement of students in their own learning;
3 adjusting teaching to take account of the results of assessment;
4 recognition of the profound influence assessment has on the motivation and self-esteem of learners, both of which are critical influences on learning;
5 the need for students to be able to assess themselves and understand how to improve.

In order for learners to have the skills necessary to engage in this process, they need to have a metacognitive understanding of what they are learning. For this to happen, teachers and support staff need to make them aware at every stage of what they are being taught, why they are being taught it, and how they need to approach the task. These are the skills that enable us to think, rather than just recite information. These are the skills that learners, particularly those with MLD, need to be explicitly taught and to have the opportunity to frequently revisit and revise.

Issues of pace, teaching style and approach

By varying the mode of teaching and the pace of the lesson, learners of all abilities get to access materials and reinforce the skills and information being taught. For some learners, especially those with attentional difficulties, the pace of the lesson needs to be quick. For others, especially those with processing difficulties, the pace of the lesson needs to have opportunities for pre-learning, repetition and over-learning of material, or for learning to happen at a slower pace.

Therefore, by understanding the learners you have in the lesson, especially those with MLD, you can plan an effective lesson – including pace and teaching methods – to suit the needs of the individuals in the class. If you have learners who you know will struggle to keep up with the pace you have planned, they can perhaps be pre-taught by a TA or mentor so that they will be more familiar with what is coming up. They can therefore assist with the delivery of the information to other learners to sustain their attention on the task.

By varying teaching style and pace, lessons will always be interesting and novel to learners. They will find it hard to predict what they will be doing, how they will be doing it and what they will learn from it.

Task or process?

When asking for feedback on a learner's progress in a particular lesson or subject, teachers and TAs can often be heard to say, 'He's done really well; he's finished all the work'. While such positive recognition and praise is to be encouraged, the natural response to a comment such as this has to be, 'And did he understand it?'. This may sound an obvious question, but it is surprising the number of teachers who can overlook learners who do not understand what they have just been taught because the teacher is relieved to be able to tick it off the list of topics to cover.

There are often significant pressures on teachers to 'get through' the necessary material, sometimes within a very short timeframe, and often battling other factors such as Christmas activities, challenging behaviours and staff and student absence. It is understandable why some breathe a sigh of relief when they can cross one of their topics off their list.

However, if we think of our own learning, do we learn best when we are presented with something once or twice, quickly and with pressure to just complete the work? Or do we learn more effectively when we take our time, understand what we are learning, apply it to our own situation and even explain it others?

If we teach learners to just complete the task, without understanding it, we are telling them that learning is not really as important as handing something in to please your teacher. It also suggests that finishing work is the most important thing, and leads us all to a situation in which we tell our learners the 'right' answers rather than helping them to learn useful concepts or skills and relating this to the process they need to go through to arrive at the solution.

We came across this extreme example of task or process in a journal a while ago. It is perfect to include here because it sums up the essence of why rushing through work, without learners actually engaging, is ineffective:

> 'Sometimes it gets discouraging because he is asleep, but I try. I just feel like I am baby-sitting. I don't feel like I'm doing what I am supposed to be doing.'
> This instructional assistant was observed repeatedly continuing to speak to the student and presenting activity-related objects, even though it was obvious that the student was asleep.
>
> (Giangreco et al. 1997, p. 14)

While we may not have learners asleep in our classrooms, if they are daydreaming or not attending to the information presented then they will be learning as much as if they were asleep. If we have learners who do not understand how to add securely, then it would be obvious that we should focus on this before teaching them about Pythagoras, yet there are many learners who do not have the core concepts of adding, subtracting and number value in place, and who are nevertheless being exposed to concepts and theories that are beyond them.

Therefore we need to try to resist the pressure to 'get work done', and to maintain the learning focus as much as possible. Remembering the theories and frameworks outlined above should help us to keep learning in mind.

Chapter 5

What do learners bring to the table and how can we plug the gaps?

In the previous chapter we explored different theories of learning and teaching, but what skills and competencies do our learners need to be effective and independent in their learning? Does a learner's starting point really matter, and how can we develop gaps they may have in their learning?

There are in fact many skills that are needed in order to be a successful learner. Some of these may be secure in the learners you are working with, whereas others may need work. Figure 5.1 represents the interplay between different cognitive skills, emotional skills and behaviours which impact on a learner's ability to regulate themselves in lessons. This is not an exhaustive list, but indicates that there is not one key skill or ability that is needed to enable learners to sit, listen, attend to what is going on, retain it and manipulate it for later use. There are a number of areas where learners with MLD may have difficulties and where teachers can intervene in the classroom.

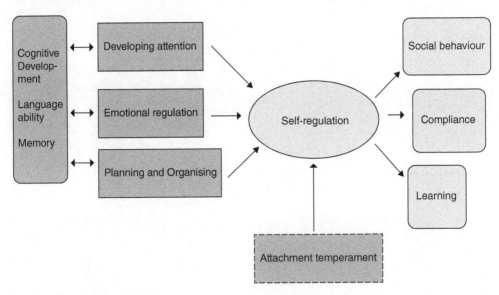

Figure 5.1   Self-regulation processes

Attention and concentration

The first key skill that learners need to acquire is the ability to attend and concentrate on what they are being taught. You may ask why attention is so vital for learning. To put it simply, if learners are not paying attention to what it is they are being taught they are unlikely to learn it.

William James (2000/1890) summarised attention as 'focalisation, concentration, consciousness are of its essence. It implies withdrawal from some things in order to deal effectively with others' (p. 404).

Attention has a number of different components and requires a number of brain regions to operate in unison. The four main aspects of attentional skill that need to be developed for active learning are:

- **Filtering attention and ignoring distractions** – being able to rapidly process information and decide if it is important to continue attending to or if it can be ignored. This also includes an ability to be able to overlook random activities in their periphery, such as people talking or movement around the room.
- **Sustaining attention** – being able to maintain focus on a specific task for sufficient time to complete it.
- **Shifting attention** – being able to move attention from one task onto another task.
- **Regulating attention** – being able to manage their attentional processes without requiring external prompts to regulate attention or shift attention between tasks.

In order for a learner to be able to regulate their attention, they need to be able to filter and sustain their attention while ignoring distractions. Learners who struggle with this will need external support to facilitate this cognitive skill.

Research has shown that the more practice we have at a skill, the less attention is needed to perform the task. For example, people who have been driving for a long time appear able to drive effortlessly while also having conversations and navigating. In comparison, new drivers have to spend so much time focusing on what they are doing in the car and what is going on around them that they often do not hear what people next to them are saying. What are the implications for those who struggle with attention and concentration in the classroom? Well, it means a learner needs to:

1 know what they need to be focusing their attention on;
2 have sufficient time to process the information and the right amount of information for their level – if it is an unfamiliar task with new ideas and concepts, they will need either longer to make sense of the information or less information to work through alone;
3 know when they need to stop;
4 have conditions that reduce distractions;
5 be aware of why they are focusing on it – if people are talking about something that we do not believe is important we won't attend to it.

Attention and concentration troubleshooter

Does the learner...	If the answer is no, you can...
know **what to focus on**?	remind them of what **exactly** they are focusing on.
have **time** to process the information?	give them **additional time** to process the information.
know how and when to **stop and re-focus**?	tell them **how long they have** and **attract their attention** when necessary – touch them, call their name, give them a visual sign.
have conditions that reduce **distractions**?	keep **noise and visual stimuli** to a minimum.
have an awareness of **why** they are focusing – why it is **relevant and important** to them?	explain **why** you are teaching it to them, and **why it is important**.

Figure 5.2 Attention and concentration troubleshooter

Strategies to develop focus and attention

Filtering attention	Reduce the amount of stimulus that learners have to filter: ■ Highlight key words/ideas. ■ Use the minimal number of sheets of paper or resources. ■ Use screens and headphones if they need to work unassisted. ■ Remove superfluous stimuli from the classroom, e.g. 'busy' displays. ■ The room should not be cluttered or too chaotic.
Sustaining attention	■ Use timers so that learners know how long they need to focus for. ■ Use their name to remind them to be on task. ■ Give them visual instructions to refer to if they lose focus. ■ Tell them what you expect them to have done in the time set. ■ Don't get them to shift the direction of their focus frequently, e.g. by having to look between the board and their work book when making notes.
Ignoring distractions	■ Reduce the number of unexpected 'surprises' that learners are exposed to – don't give unexpected tests, for example. ■ Establish a routine so they know what to expect. ■ Manage classroom behaviour and reward learners who are focused and on task. ■ When learners are settled, try not to break their focus unless the time is up or they are on the wrong track.
Regulating attention	■ Remind learners that they are in charge of their focus. ■ Make sure they are aware of when they are off task. ■ Give learners tasks that they are able to focus on – if they lose focus after 10 minutes, expecting them to focus for 50 minutes is unrealistic.

Figure 5.3 Strategies to develop focus and attention

Learner focus sheet

Name _____

Listen hard and use this sheet to note down key
information from the lesson today.

What?	
Who?	
Where?	
When?	
How?	

Figure 5.4a Learner focus sheet

Learner focus sheet

Name _____

Listen hard and use this sheet to note down key
information from the lesson today.

Figure 5.4b Adaptable learner focus sheet

Memory

Memory is something we often take for granted. It's only when we find ourselves forgetting something at the supermarket, or when we pop upstairs only to forget why we went there, that we realise that we use a range of strategies to assist our ability to retain information on a daily basis.

Before we explore ways of assisting learners with MLD who have memory issues, it is important to clarify how our memory actually works. Memory is a process, not a discrete skill, and requires a range of other cognitive skills to assist it.

In order to remember something we need to:

1 perceive that something is important;
2 attend to the information;
3 make it meaningful – link it to previous knowledge (akin to a spider's web) so we can place it in storage;
4 put it in a sensible place – much like a filing cabinet;
5 have a way to find it – we refer to this as retrieval.

We have different types of memory depending on what it is we are doing:

■ long-term memory for previously learnt facts and skills;
■ autobiographical memory – for events in our life;
■ short-term memory – for immediate things that we need to decide if it is relevant and worth focusing more attention on;
■ working memory – putting something on one side while we adjust it and tweak it.

The most relevant memory stores for learning are short-term memory and working memory. Baddeley and Hitch (1974) proposed a very influential model of working memory, as shown in Figure 5.5:

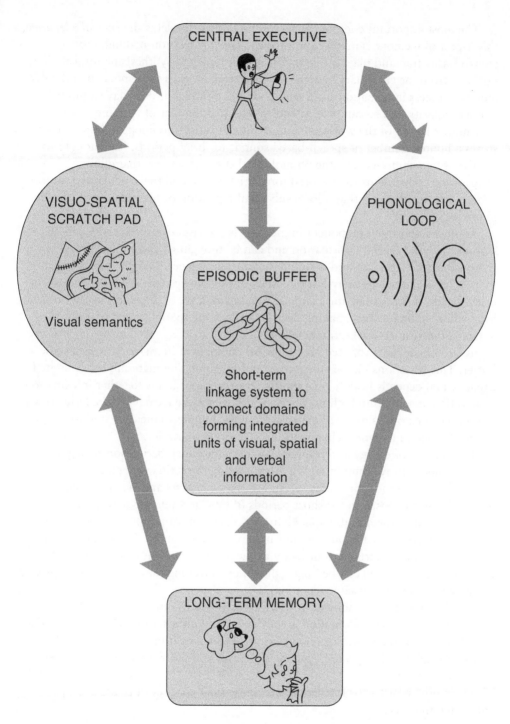

Figure 5.5 Working memory processes

The most important component according to their model is the *central executive*; this aspect of memory is involved in problem-solving/decision-making. It also controls attention and plays a major role in planning and synthesising information, not only from the subsidiary systems but also from long-term memory. It is flexible and can process information from any modality, although it does have a limited storage capacity and so can only attend to a limited number of elements at one time.

Another aspect of the working memory model is the phonological loop, which stores a limited number of speech-based sounds for brief periods. It is thought to consist of two components – the phonological store (inner ear) that allows acoustically coded items to be stored for a brief period and the articulatory control process (the inner voice) that allows sub-vocal repetition of the items stored in the phonological store.

Another important component in memory is the visuo-spatial scratch pad; it stores visual and spatial information and can be thought of as an inner eye. It is responsible for setting up and manipulating mental images. Like the phonological loop, it has a limited capacity but the limits of the two systems are independent. In other words, it is possible, for example, to rehearse a set of digits in the phonological loop while simultaneously making decisions about the spatial layout of a set of letters in the visuo-spatial scratch pad.

In 2000 Baddeley proposed an additional component in memory: the episodic buffer. This is responsible for integrating and manipulating material; it has limited capacity and depends heavily on executive processing. It binds together information from different sources into chunks or episodes, hence the term 'episodic'. One of its important functions is to recall material from the long-term memory and to integrate it into short-term memory when working memory requires it.

The amount of energy and resource we invest in remembering something depends on how important we think it is. We are not going to retain every piece of information we come into contact with, but there are facts and events which we have only been exposed to for short periods of time and yet stay with us forever. Our brain works unbelievably quickly to process the information and decide if it is worth storing or not – the purpose of our short-term memory. For learners with MLD, this can be a particular difficulty as the length of time it can take them to process the information can be longer than most, meaning they are unable to place it in the rehearsal store for later retention.

If you consider for a moment how we are exposed to different types of information, auditory information is the one type of information which we are able to hold on to for the shortest period of time. As soon as it has been heard, it vanishes – unless it is repeated – whereas pictures and written words can be seen for as long as needed.

Therefore, in order for learners to maximise their chances of remembering something they need to:

- see it visually – through demonstrations, pictures, photographs, film and diagrams;
- experience it themselves through role play, action, experiments, etc.;
- understand why it is important and meaningful;
- have repeated access to the target information.

Perception

Learners need to be able to extract information from the sources they are given. This includes visual, auditory and kinaesthetic information. In addition to identifying the information source, learners also need to process the information and combine it with other sources at the same time to form a complete representation.

As teaching becomes more interactive, learners have to process and attend to a greater number of sources of information at once and process them more quickly than previous generations might have had to. This places greater demands on their cognitive capacity and we are often oblivious to the speed at which we expect learners to keep up with us.

Often learners have a preference for one or two modalities (for example, visual and kinaesthetic, or just visual). However, the traditional model of teaching in secondary schools is one which relies heavily on the auditory modality, even though we know that this mode of information is accessible for the shortest amount of time, as well as being less likely to be retained in the learner's memory. This is particularly relevant for learners with MLD.

Strategies to develop memory and perceptual skills

Memory can be an area of real difficulty for some learners with MLD. Difficulties with retaining information can have a real impact on learning processes, as well as impacting on confidence and self-esteem.

It is important to use a range of modes to present information to learners so that they have a range of opportunities to see the meaning and hold on to the information. In addition, by using various mediums to present information, you are increasing the likelihood that the perceptual system will pick it up and link it together – a picture along with music is far easier to recall than just music or a picture.

Use pictures, sounds, music and movement to convey your ideas. One medium alone is boring and easily forgettable, but varying and combining mediums makes the ideas more memorable.

When we talk about supporting memory, what we mean is finding ways of increasing storage and improving retrieval. We can do this primarily in two ways:

- learn the information over and over again;
- learn the information in relation to other knowledge we already have.

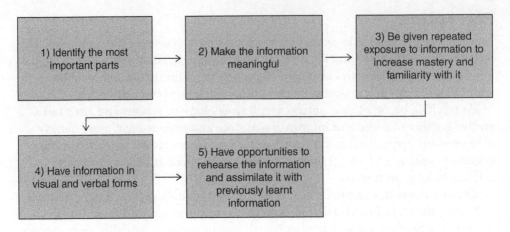

Figure 5.6 Five key stages for learning and remembering new information

Examples of ways to do this are:

- mind maps;
- precision teaching;
- timelines;
- memory games – shopping list, the game 'whispers', under the blanket;
- sentence/idea starters;
- visual cues – pictures, lists of things to do, charts;
- auditory cues – sounds, music;
- olfactory cues – regular smells in the classroom;
- create visual webs for new ideas or vocabulary to show how it links in with previous knowledge.

It is also worth encouraging learners to engage with new topics on a sensory level. It can be worth using an input grid such as the one overleaf. This helps the learner to think about all aspects of the topic and to link ideas to a number of sensory inputs, so becomes easier to recall.

Sensory input grid

Name _____

Topic: _____	
Sight	
Sound	
Smell	
Taste	
Touch	

Figure 5.7   Sensory input grid

Understanding ourselves as learners

Often when people talk about cognitive skills, they are referring to the concept of 'intelligence'. Intelligence itself is not a measurable, observable fact – it is an abstract concept that we have tried to capture through the use of standardised tests and assessments.

These various tests and assessments give us the impression that cognition and intelligence are discrete and measurable characteristics. However, the reality is that our cognition and intelligence are factors of both our biology and environment. Our perception, attention, memory and engagement are the direct result of where we are and what we are being asked to do.

The true measure of intelligence is in fact our ability to be creative when resolving problems by drawing upon previous knowledge and assessing the situation. In order to be effective problem solvers, we need to be able to:

- understand what the problem is that we have to solve;
- select only the relevant pieces of information to help us solve the problem;
- create a theory of how we can solve it – a hypothesis;
- have a system/process in place to work through;
- be accurate and precise;
- be able to generate alternative solutions if necessary;
- be able to transfer skills from other situations and generalise our knowledge to be adaptable;
- review our performances and reflect on what we did well, what helped us and what we need to do better next time.

If learners are conscious of what they are doing, they are more likely to be engaging their thoughts in the process and therefore are more likely to be developing their metacognitive skills. If learners are not aware of what they are doing, they won't be able to utilise their thinking skills and so will be learning things at a superficial level.

The skills linked to understanding ourselves as learners are called metacognitive skills, and increased skill in this area leads to increased ability in transferring skills between topics and disciplines. It is these skills that we are attempting to activate when we use the *Assessment for Learning* strategies that we discussed earlier.

In order for learners to develop these skills, they need to be taught how to think and justify their answers – both when they are right and when they are wrong. This is the skill which is most substantially linked to independent working.

Logic

What is logic? It is often associated with complex problem-solving and reasoning, but it does not have to be. In its most simplistic form, logic is about recognising things are different or the same and using this information to distinguish between the two. As young learners, we start using logic to understand concepts such as number, shapes, colours etc. We start building up models of how to sort and match items from different groups from an early age and we build on these skills as we progress through childhood.

The varying skills involved in logic are:

- comparing items and concepts;
- classifying and grouping items or concepts;
- the ability to conserve constancies – this means to be able to recognise what characteristics are constant for concepts and items;
- the ability to see the cause and effect relationships between items and concepts;
- using analogy (*a* is to *b* as *c* is to *d*);
- using inference (if these two are *x* then this must be *y*).

Being logical means applying a system to rule out certain answers and to arrive at a more justified and rational solution. By being logical, we are able to apply a system for attending to and storing information, which supports our memory and attentional skills and means we are more likely to retrieve information accurately at will, rather than by a random trial-and-error approach.

Strategies to develop logic and metacognition

Suggested questions

- Where did you find that information?
- How did you know that was the right answer?
- What information did you use that helped you?
- What information did you find relevant?
- What other ways could we solve this?
- Does the answer still fit if we add this piece of information?
- What information do you need to answer the question?
- What information are we missing?
- Is there any information that does not fit?
- Can we order the information so it makes more sense?
- What information gave you that answer?
- What should you do first?
- What will you do next?
- Do you know what information you need?
- Do you understand the question?
- How much time should you allocate per question?
- What key words and phrases do you need to include?
- How will you know if you are on the right track?
- How many examples and pieces of evidence do you need to give?

Figure 5.8 Suggested questions

Ask yourself whether there are questions that the learner consistently struggles to answer. If so, these are the areas they need to ask for support with. These questions will help them to start planning their answers. When they plan their answers and method of approach, encourage them to write down all their thinking so they have a record they can refer back to at a later date.

When helping a learner to develop their logic skills it is important to get them to see the process and procedures involved in finding out the right answer. This can be done by:

- encouraging comparison;
- encouraging sorting and grouping;
- getting them to define concepts, for example what makes a square a square, etc.;
- looking at cause and effect – what did we do to make this happen? What happens if you do this?;
- using analogies;
- encouraging them to use inference to further the information they have been given (for example, telling them about a location and characters, and asking them what is going on).

The following figures (5.9, 5.10, 5.11 and 5.12) provide a range of structures which can be used to support a learner to organise and plan the information they have in order to construct and evidence their views.

Similarities and differences

Name _____

In what ways are these two things **the same**?	In what ways are they **different**?

Figure 5.9 Similarities and differences

	Describe A	Describe B	Compare similarities	Contrast differences	Evaluate/ analyse Why?
What?					
Who?					
Where?					
How?					
Key features					
Key words					

Figure 5.10 Comparison grid

	For	Against
Argument 1		
Evidence 1		
Argument 2		
Evidence 2		
Argument 3		
Evidence 3		

Figure 5.11 Evidence-based grid for and against an argument

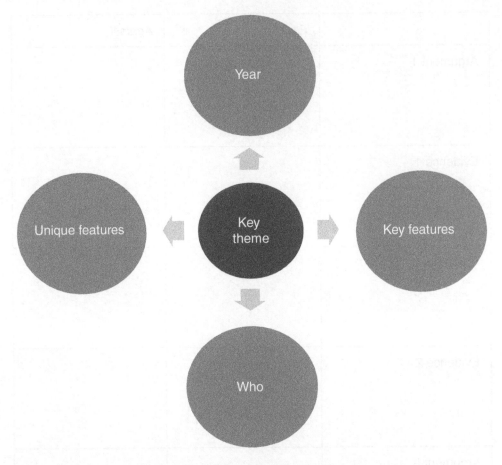

Figure 5.12 Spider diagram to link pieces of information with a key theme

- Explain exactly what is needed and show learners examples of what the finished article/product should look like.
- Prioritise key information and encourage learners to think about what knowledge is essential to complete the task.
- What is their hypothesis:
  - How can they test it out and how many ways can they think of to do so? For example, how many number bonds to 10 are there?
  - Do all triangles have angles which add up to 180 degrees?
  - Do all words have vowels in them?
  - Are all types of wood the same? And so on.
- Give them a plan or system to aid their structuring of work, such as:
  - sentence starters;
  - writing frames;
  - comic strips;
  - numbering of points or stages to work through.
- Remind learners to be accurate and precise in their working. For example, they need to be made aware that errors in measuring and recording in lessons can

have a significant impact on the outcome. This means that the wrong spelling can change the entire meaning of a sentence and varying the amount of ingredients mixed together can produce a completely different meal to the one which was intended.

- Link to previous learning and to future learning.
- Encourage reflection and descriptions about what the learner has done to solve the problem:
  - What could have been better and what worked well?
  - Can they describe the process they worked through or did they just 'know the answer'?
  - If they just knew it, give them cues to think about – such as how did they know it was x, which one had to go there, what is the same about these two, what is different, and so on.

Social interaction

You may ask why social skills and interactions are included in a book about MLD as skills that are needed for effective learning. The answer is simple. Our brains have developed as a result of interactions with others. Evolution has determined that we are stronger as a team than individually and the same is true in learning.

We learn from what we see others do and the responses they make. We learn from other's mistakes and we assimilate information from other's experiences into our own. For this reason, learners need to learn how to interact appropriately with their peers so that they can effectively cooperate as part of a team.

Being a team member includes being able to **listen** to other's ideas and respond appropriately, **put forward separate ideas** that may be different from the ones previously expressed, and to **compromise** to obtain a mutually satisfactory solution.

Components of successful interactions include:

- reading facial expressions;
- reading visual cues and information;
- being able to ask and answer questions appropriately, providing sufficient information without going over the top;
- being able to organise information;
- being able to sequence information into logical orders;
- inferring what someone may think about something from where their eye gaze is;
- being able to manage physical proximity appropriate to the social situation;
- being flexible enough so that they can compromise when others do not agree with their view.

If learners struggle with one or more of these, they will need to be explicitly taught these skills and they will also need to be told why they are being taught them.

This can be done through interventions such as behaviour mapping and prescriptive individual scripts to illustrate the key skill.

Story scripts

If learners are struggling to understand social rules, they need to be taught them explicitly and provided with a reason as to why they are important. Social scripts can be created which outline the key skills to develop and why, for example:

Using kind words and voices

In school we expect students to use kind words and voices.

This makes teachers and other students feel safe and respected.

Other people will use kind words and voices when they talk to you.

You will try to use kind words and voices when talking to other students and to adults.

The script can be used with the learner every day and adapted to their developing needs. If appropriate, pictures or photographs can be used alongside the social script to reinforce the desired behaviour. We are wanting to tell learners what we expect, so they should be written and phrased in ways which mean the learner is clear about what they should do, not about what they should not do.

Visual alternatives, such as story boards, can be created to explore a learner's interpretation of a situation they may have found difficult and alternative endings can be explored by using thought bubbles and speech bubbles.

Question starters

The diagrams in Figure 5.13 can be used to support learners in formulating different questions to ask each other during tasks and topics when they are unsure of what they can ask.

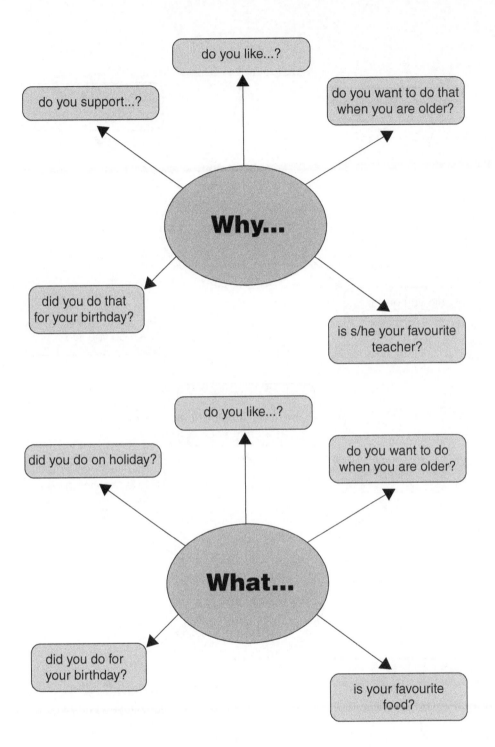

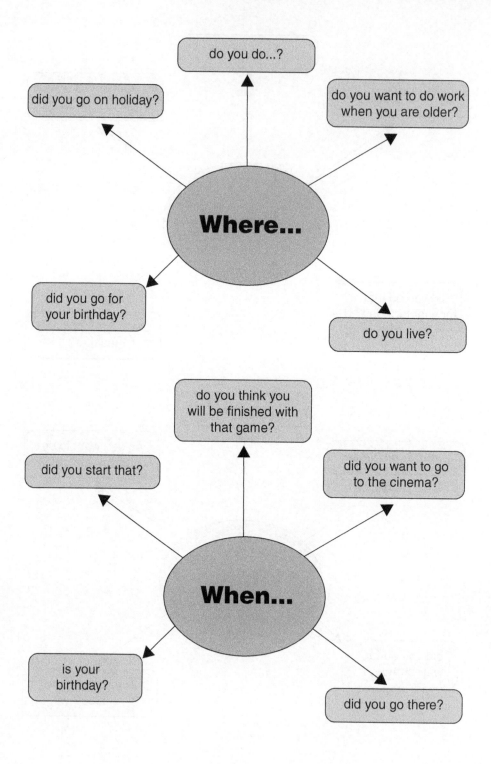

do you do...?

did you go on holiday?

do you want to do work when you are older?

Where...

did you go for your birthday?

do you live?

do you think you will be finished with that game?

did you start that?

did you want to go to the cinema?

When...

is your birthday?

did you go there?

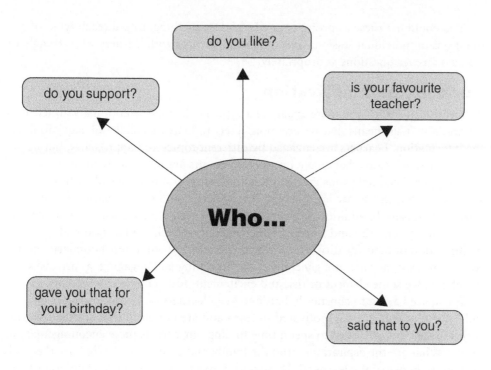

Figure 5.13 Question starter spider diagrams

You could use these as prompts in whole-class teaching, to pre-teach types of questions in individual sessions or within small groups with learners who struggle to ask and answer questions appropriately.

Curiosity and motivation

As mentioned earlier, the more engaging a topic is, the more emotionally attached we are to it. This means that we are more likely to increase recall and acquisition of the information. Learners are engaged by different topics and approaches, but in general, active lessons that create unexpected results are more likely to raise curiosity. Predictable lessons give learners the impression that they already know what is coming and so are less likely to pay attention and recall what occurred during the lesson. In addition, learners who are in their adolescence are more drawn to risk-taking activities and learning which encourages self-exploration and confirmation of their identity. Tasks which encourage them to test boundaries and to explore who they are, are generally more appealing and engaging, as are tasks which involve some element of risk and excitement, for example experiments.

If you are having to constantly battle to keep learners on board, then it is an indicator that they are not motivated to learn and are not curious about their world. If this is the case, you need to spend time finding out why. Is there encouragement at home? What are the aspirations from the family and community? What are the goals and future hopes of the learners? These questions can be a useful starting point for tailoring learning to topics that are likely to engage and interest them, and to elicit a greater degree of curiosity and motivation.

Language

Language in the classroom is the key medium through which we impart knowledge from one person to another. This can be done via aural or visual means but both of these rely on the learner's ability to process information accurately and then use that information to either construct a response or to store it for later usage.

When working in schools, we often unconsciously adopt a different style of spoken and written language than we would usually use when speaking, for example, to our own children, or to a friend's children. For example, we tend to use subject-specific language and often a more formal tone than we might use in our usual interactions.

We don't often notice that we are using more formal or complex language. When we ourselves were pupils in school, we were usually taught in this 'schoolese' and often we personally responded well to this type of communication, hence why we are now working in schools ourselves! However, there are and always have been learners who are not able to access information that is presented in this way, during our own schooldays and in the classrooms we work in now.

Learners with MLD will often have a less sophisticated bank of language to draw upon both when they listen to/read information (receptive language) and when they express themselves in writing or in speech (expressive language).

Consider, for example, the following instruction, which could be heard in any science classroom in the UK and beyond:

> You need to very carefully insert the tongs into the end of the beaker, making sure please that you don't allow your tongs to touch the liquid until I instruct you to.

At first glance this seems relatively simple as a spoken instruction – certainly we, as academically competent adult learners, are unlikely to have difficulties understanding what is meant by this, or using this information to follow the instruction.

However if we deconstruct the language of this sentence, we can see that we actually require a number of quite advanced skills to make sense of it.

We need to know the meanings of quite complex words such as 'insert', 'allow', 'liquid' and 'instruct', and of subject-specific words such as 'tongs' and 'beaker'. You need to be able not only to know and recognise the meanings of these words, but also to hold all of these meanings in your working memory at the same time as you make sense of the relationships between each of these concepts. In addition, you need to understand the construction of a lengthy and complex sentence and be able to discriminate which information is important to the meaning (for example, 'DON'T allow your tongs to touch the liquid'), from which information is less important ('please'). Therefore we can see that the way we use language is often a barrier for learners who have MLD as well as other additional needs such as speech, language and communication needs, English as an Additional Language, or autistic spectrum conditions.

Let's now imagine that the same information was given in a different way:

> Watch me now, and I will show you what to do. I am going to call this blue stuff 'liquid'. Put your tongs inside the glass beaker. Don't let the tongs touch the blue liquid yet.

In this instruction, the information given is almost exactly the same, but it is immediately much more accessible to the learners. The language is simpler and meanings are supported by simple adjectives such as the words 'glass' and 'blue'. The sentences are shorter and grammatically simpler, and so the transmission of meaning relies less upon the learners' understanding of syntax. Important technical words (such as 'liquid') are explicitly pointed out and explained before they are used. Also the teacher is using a visual reinforcement (showing learners what to do while explaining), which means that the key information is transmitted in two ways – through seeing what needs to be done, and through hearing the language instruction.

It is vital when working with learners who have MLD that we adjust our language accordingly. Indeed, these strategies for clear communication benefit all learners, not just those with MLD, and are of particular value to learners with additional needs such as those outlined above.

It seems logical that if instructions and information are not accessible, then nothing further can be done with them.

Summary

All these skills and requirements for learning have been presented discretely; however, they are needed in combination to be effective. We learn as a process:

- Information comes to us in a range of ways – via our perceptual skills, our receptive language skills, our attention, and our motivation and curiosity.
- Our elaboration skills include our metacognitive skills, our memory, our attention, our desire to persevere and continue even when it is hard, and our reasoning and logical skills.
- Our output consists of communicating an answer or response to someone using our expressive language skills and our social skills. It is often assumed that if a learner cannot express their answer they have not understood the task. However, it is important to assess all stages of learning, as it may be that they simply do not have the vocabulary to explain their ideas or understanding.

Chapter 6

How can teachers personalise and differentiate for learning?

Differentiation – what is it?

Differentiation is the process by which teachers (as in anyone imparting knowledge and developing a learner's skills) adapt the materials, delivery and content to enable a learner to access the intended message. Where there is excellent differentiation, learners are able to acquire information more independently and develop a clearer understanding of key concepts. In this way they are involved and included in the lesson. Very few would argue that differentiation and personalisation are not a good idea, or are not needed for learners in their classrooms and schools.

However, you will probably identify with having regularly seen (or even taught) lessons where there is inadequate, or non-existent, differentiation. In these lessons, all learners will often be working on the same learning objectives, through completing the same tasks, at the same or at a similar pace. Some learners will be struggling, some will be managing just fine, while others will be bored as there is inadequate challenge for them. In the best case, learners will be quietly occupied with the tasks they've been given; in most cases, however, in such a lesson the majority will fail to make tangible progress, and some may 'act out' their boredom or frustration with behaviours which provide an immediate diversion.

This leads, then, to the question of why so many lessons continue to be undifferentiated. There are many reasons why this is the case. Time is certainly one of these: a teacher's workload is enormous and they already spend a significant amount of time planning their lessons on top of their usual teaching day.

Often memories of teacher training on 'differentiation' conjure up visions of preparing three versions of every worksheet – 'foundation', 'main' and 'higher' – and of planning late into the night to get all this done!

However the very best and inclusive practice, with engaging, effective and sustainable strategies for differentiation, is not about preparing lots of versions of every resource. Rather, it is about investing thought and energy into how a lesson will be made accessible to all learners, making sure that any additional resources that are prepared are shared and can be re-used, which will likely include co-planning and sharing materials at a departmental level.

To illustrate this, Figure 6.1 shows a range of approaches that a school or a subject department might take to differentiation and personalisation:

Greatest planning time		Least planning time
Teachers differentiate on an individual basis as part of their regular lesson planning. Resources are sometimes shared with other teachers, but generally each plans for their own classes.	Teachers differentiate on an individual basis as part of their regular lesson planning and differentiated resources are purposely saved electronically alongside schemes of work so that a bank of these is built up, over time. These materials can easily be adapted for future learners and groups of learners, thereby saving planning time.	Schemes of work are planned at departmental level to always include a basic level of differentiation which will enable a greater number of learners to access learning. This might include, for example, a core expectation that every scheme of work includes: ■ writing frames for written tasks; ■ key word lists with picture clues for each topic; ■ visual reinforcement such as picture clues and key words highlighted on all worksheets and PowerPoint slides. Where individual learners need greater or different differentiation than this, then materials can be added to the bank of resources and re-used as appropriate.

Figure 6.1 A range of approaches towards differentiation and personalisation

What we are arguing is that teachers need to work together and plan collaboratively if they are to differentiate effectively. Not only does this allow for time saving by sharing resources, it also allows colleagues to share ideas, to develop best practice and to develop consistency rather than isolated 'spots' of good practice.

Some schools and academies also utilise the expertise of TAs to plan differentiated materials for learners with additional needs. Clearly there are benefits to this approach, given that TAs often have most contact with individual learners, and work with them across a range of subjects, so have privileged and unique knowledge of the learners they support. In addition, planning time can sometimes be included on TAs' timetables so that they can actively perform this role.

There are however, also clear disadvantages to this model, not least that it removes some of the professional responsibility for learners' progress and planning from the subject teacher. Recent frameworks such as the OFSTED *School Inspection Handbook* 2015, the Teachers' Professional Standards 2011 and the Code of Practice for SEND 2014 are very clear that the teacher is responsible for the planning and progress of learners with SEND. In addition, a TA is less likely to have specialist subject knowledge and to know the 'core' concepts that learners need to learn, and therefore resources prepared by TAs may focus on ideas which are not key concepts. Furthermore, this model reinforces the sense that TAs are responsible for learners with SEN – that they are someone 'different' from the mainstream and needing something which the subject teacher cannot provide. This strategy therefore should be used with caution.

Research on the views of learners with MLD has found that they want work which is challenging but which is at the right level for them to complete more or less independently. This is where effective differentiation comes in – when done well and sensitively it has a myriad of benefits both for learners, and for the adults who work with them.

Differentiation will vary greatly depending on the needs of the learners, the subject, and the interests, learning and teaching styles of teachers. There are, however, some clear elements of great practice which every teacher can adopt in order to provide excellent differentiation. Most of these do not take lots of extra planning time, or where there is additional planning, this can be approached through the collaborative approach mentioned above. Generally, they are just about thoughtful adjustments to lesson planning and teaching within the lesson.

Issues for consideration:

Why differentiate?

Eight great reasons why it's worth it...

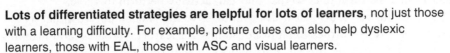

Learners with additional needs **will not always be able to access learning** unless you differentiate for them – their success, now and in the future, is in your hands (but that doesn't mean it has to be onerous...).

Lots of differentiated strategies are helpful for lots of learners, not just those with a learning difficulty. For example, picture clues can also help dyslexic learners, those with EAL, those with ASC and visual learners.

If we rely solely on TA support to 'get them through the lesson', we are likely to end up with learners who **have completed some work but who have understood little**.

Learners are much more likely to enjoy their time with you if they can understand the key learning points and take full part in the lesson.

If we don't differentiate, the learners in our lessons are much more likely to display **challenging behaviours** – whether through boredom, to distract attention from the fact that they can't understand or as a reflection of how frustrated they feel.

We need learners to leave school **knowing that they are successful learners**. This will only happen if they are provided with learning activities that they can do. If they can't access learning, then their view of themselves will be one of failure.

Learners will only develop an understanding of how to learn if they are given the space to do this. Work needs to be at the right level for them so they can access it without constant adult help.

Great differentiation is one of the things that can **make our schools, academies and individual lessons 'outstanding'**. OFSTED, for example, says it is looking at:

> the extent to which teachers' expectations, reflected in their teaching and planning, including curriculum planning, are sufficiently high to extend the previous knowledge, skills and understanding of all pupils in a range of lessons and activities over time

> the extent to which well-judged teaching strategies, including setting challenging tasks matched to pupils' learning needs, successfully engage all pupils in their learning

> the extent to which teachers enable pupils to develop the skills to learn for themselves...

> the quality of teaching and other support provided for pupils with a range of aptitudes and needs, including disabled pupils and those who have special educational needs, so that their learning improves.

Figure 6.2 Why differentiate?

Great practice in differentiation and personalisation

1. Practical learning

We all love learning about things first-hand through doing, rather than learning second-hand through reading about it in someone else's words. Practical learning is a fantastic way of encouraging engagement and accessibility for all learners, particularly those who have learning difficulties but also those with attentional difficulties.

Activities such as:

- role plays;
- practicals;
- constructing models;
- fieldwork;
- experiments;

are all fantastic ways of making learning more accessible by removing the abstraction of learning from 'second-hand information' and bringing learning to the 'here and now'.

2. Group work

Group work allows for learners to take on the subject matter and enter into interaction with and about it. In well-planned group work, learners get to discuss, debate, argue, collaborate, develop, evaluate, critique and articulate a shared experience of the learning. For those with learning difficulties, the support of peers can offer valuable scaffolding and reassurance, and can encourage greater confidence and inclusion than working alone or with a TA.

It is vital that groups are well-planned in advance of the lesson if they are to be successful – it is worth considering whether groups will be peer groupings, ability groupings, mixed-ability or hand-picked according to the needs of the individuals. All of these groupings have their own pros and cons, so it is worth investing time in considering these in order for the group dynamics to be positive and successful. Too many teachers have had to 'abandon' group work with diverse classes because it has been unsuccessful at the first try, when in fact it has the potential to make a very positive impact on learning progress and engagement.

It is also worth considering roles within the group – will you allocate these (often this reduces opportunities for conflict) or will the group allocate these to themselves? Often it can be useful to allocate specific roles and responsibilities so that everyone feels valued and no one person is allowed to dominate. Usefully roles might include:

- scribe,
- chairperson,
- feedback leader,
- sparring partner (voicing challenge and argument – ideal for a more able learner),
- counter-spar (voicing counter-challenge and counter-argument) and so on.

These roles and their functions will need to be explicitly taught so that all learners understand and share expectations. In itself, this is a vital skill needed in the workplace, and a number of learners have difficulty collaborating in groups simply because they have never been taught how to work in this way effectively before.

Group work is at its most successful when timings, expectations and learning outcomes are clear. Spend some time at the beginning explaining not only what the task is, but also:

- why they are doing this,
- what 'work' (outcome) they are expected to achieve in order to evidence their learning,
- what expectations you have in terms of noise, and language to be used (formal, chatty, respectful?)
- what this will sound like (what words and phrases might you expect to hear?).

3. Individual explanations

When talking about their learning, this is often the strategy which learners with learning difficulties cite as most useful in the classroom. They particularly value a teacher who checks whether they understand, is patient with them when they don't, and who will explain and show them what they have to do in words they can understand.

The most fantastic thing about this is that it doesn't require lots of additional planning, resources or photocopying! All it needs is a teacher or TA who knows their learners and their learning needs, knows which of these may need additional explanations at times, and understands which learners are likely to ask for these and which are not likely to.

Using target learners to recap what the task is can also be a useful way of checking their understanding and sharing a recap with the rest of the class. The chances are, if one learner has not understood the task, others might not have either.

4. Accessible text

In most classrooms there are likely to be a number of learners whose reading ability is lower than that of their peers, and among these are likely to be those with MLD. This means that many texts which are used in these lessons – textbooks, worksheets, web pages, among others – will be too difficult for these learners to decode and/or to understand.

It is really important, therefore, that written text is made accessible in every classroom. There are many ways in which this can be done:

a One really effective way of making text more accessible is to include little pictures that illustrate the main points or ideas. This is a very simple but incredibly valuable strategy. As an example of how powerful this can be, take a few moments to read and absorb the four important messages in the table below:

Halten Sie die Fenster geschlossen.
No se puede comer!
Les chiens sont interdits à l'intérieur.
Папярэджанне - таксічныя газы!

Unless you are skilled in understanding German, Spanish, French or Belarusian, chances are you struggled with grasping the meaning of these sentences. You may have read and re-read them, looking for words that you recognised in order to get an idea of what they were about. If you were doing this in class, however, and re-reading information in your first language because you have a literacy or learning difficulty, the class would most likely be moving on quickly before you had a chance to work out what was meant.

Let's try it again:

Halten Sie die Fenster geschlossen.	
No se permite comer.	
Les chiens sont interdits à l'intérieur.	
Папярэджанне - таксічныя газы!	

It is likely that, just by the addition of these four picture clues, you will have at least a basic grasp of what each sentence means. This is therefore a very easy way in which teachers can make information on PowerPoints and worksheets more accessible, not only to learners who have MLD but also to those who have EAL or dyslexia.

b Printed information can be made more accessible by paying attention to the font style and size. Traditional academic fonts such as Times New Roman are visually more complex and can therefore be more difficult to decode than, for example, Arial and Comic Sans. Similarly, slightly larger font sizes such as 12 and 14 point tend to be more accessible than 8 and 10 point. Line spacing of 1.5 or 2 lines means the text looks less cluttered on the page.

c	Some learners find that text on pastel-coloured paper is easier to read than text printed on pure white. This is believed to be because of the visual glare and very sharp contrast of black on white. It is worth having conversations with learners about which colour they find easiest to read from, because the improvement can be very marked for some learners. Coloured perspex rulers (sometimes called 'dyslexia rulers') are another way of ensuring that the learner can access text on their preferred colour background, and reduces the margin for error when teachers forget to copy onto coloured paper.

d	Another useful strategy is to highlight key words in the text before giving it to the learner. These might include:

- technical or subject-specific words or phrases which the learner needs in order to grasp the text's meaning;
- words which are likely to be new to the learner (or to the whole class);
- longer or more complex words which the learner will struggle to read (these can be broken into 'chunks' with each chunk being highlighted in a different colour).

This strategy is most useful when the highlighted words are pre-taught and explained to the class, so that meanings are clear before the text is approached. This is a strategy which can be helpful for the whole class and therefore teachers might consider preparing a text in this way and then colour-copying it so that all learners have access to the highlighted words in case they should need them. Equally, though, there are times where teaching assistants might highlight a text in this way as a form of 'on-the-spot' differentiation.

e	Another strategy is to reduce the level of demand of the text. One way in which this can be done is by rewriting and simplifying the text so that:

- the sentences are shorter and simpler;
- the font is clear and unfussy, and at least 12 point;
- language is made as simple as possible;
- any challenging words are supported by picture clues;
- the most important words and information are highlighted or underlined;
- text is split into chunks by using bullet points, text boxes, simple diagrams, and pictures with captions.

Adapting texts is a strategy that might usefully be approached at departmental level so that these texts can be shared among colleagues, as it is time-consuming to try to adapt every text in this way as part of your daily planning.

f	Another way to reduce the level of demand of the text is to reduce the amount of text that the learner or group of learners have to read (two key paragraphs rather than six, for example). This can be slightly more difficult to build into whole-class teaching but can be used when learners are reading and working on text in small groups, for example. The reduced version will need to be carefully prepared to ensure that it covers the main learning points of the enlarged text, otherwise the learners could end up only reading an introductory paragraph but none of the key content of the text!

g One further way to make text more accessible is to consider group reading and discussion. This could include structured roles such as readers, note-takers, discussion leaders and so on. Where groups are sensitively selected and the task is well-planned and set up, this can enable real collaboration in which learners provide support and challenge for each other.

What is important when adjusting the text components is that the cognitive demands remain appropriate for the cognitive abilities of the learner.

Ways to support learners with reading difficulties:

■ Information is pre-recorded onto a dictaphone, perhaps by a TA, older 'peer buddy' or learning mentor.
■ The learner is provided with a reading pen – these are commercially available and 'read' text aloud by scanning the text.
■ Shared reading aloud – in small groups, with peers or with a member of staff.
■ Text is simplified into less complex language (reading age websites can be useful in gauging the level of difficulty of a piece of text).
■ The learner is given the text with key words already highlighted.
■ The learner is given the text with picture clues included for key words and concepts.

---

5. Giving information clearly

One very simple way to differentiation, and one of the most effective, is to make sure that you are communicating key ideas and information as effectively as possible. This is particularly the case when you are communicating information verbally.

Figure 6.3 provides a reminder for staff of ways to make sure that your talk is as clear as possible.

Talking clearly: A guide for staff

Use these simple strategies to make sure that you are communicating as clearly as possible in the classroom.

Keep sentences as short as possible.

Give information directly, e.g. 'You need to sit down in your chair now please' rather than 'There shouldn't be anyone wandering around the room and chatting right now'.

Bring in the reinforcements. Display key points with pictures on the board as you talk.

Explain any new or complex words as you use them – don't assume learners know them.

Repeat key words and phrases as you talk.

Check that your learners understand what you have said to them. Ask them to explain it back to you, or to the person next to them, or to note it on a sticky note or in their book. Check their understanding by asking them to explain it in their own words so that they don't just repeat back what you've told them.

Figure 6.3 Giving information clearly

This is just as important when we present written information. Often, secondary textbooks are written in a style which is far too complex for lots of learners in our classrooms. In many cases, not only is the language too difficult but the reading age is also too high unless we are teaching higher sets.

Here is an example from a popular history revision website:

Disease

Knowledge about disease increased rapidly and significantly in the 19th century.

Louis Pasteur discovered, using a swan-necked flask, that germs cause disease. Before he made this discovery, doctors had noticed bacteria, but they wrongly believed it was the disease that caused the bacteria – the so-called theory of 'spontaneous generation' – rather than the other way round.

One of the spin-offs of Pasteur's discovery was the pasteurisation of milk. Pasteurisation prevented milk from going sour by killing the germs and sealing it from the air.

This text is intended for students of GCSE History, who will usually be aged between 14 and 16 years. However, it has a reading age of over 17 years, meaning that it is likely to be beyond the easy reach of most learners aged 14–16, let alone those with any kind of literacy or learning difficulty. Many learners in our schools will therefore struggle to access this type of academic text, even when they would have been able to understand the core ideas.

With this in mind, we need to consider quite carefully: What are the key pieces of information that we are wanting the learners to extract from this? How can they find this in complex information, as demonstrated above? The answer is we have to show them what the key pieces of information are by highlighting them, and we have to adjust some of the material we present to them to accommodate this.

6. Learning objectives

When thinking about differentiation, teachers need to be very clear about the main learning points of the lesson, i.e. what is the purpose of the lesson? This is where strong and crisply written differentiated learning objectives are crucial, since in effect the whole lesson should 'hang off' these objectives. Where this doesn't happen, lessons often end up having a 'task focus' rather than a 'cognitive focus' – so attention is given to 'what work will they do?' or 'how will we fill the time up?' rather than 'what will they learn?'.

Schools often have their own models and norms for writing learning objectives, but well-differentiated lessons are likely to feature the following:

- There is a range of learning objectives which build on each other and increase in level of challenge. Learners should have a learning objective which is achievable yet challenging for them. It might be that you want to give one objective for each National Curriculum level or GCSE grade, or you may want to build in challenge through the use of Bloom's Taxonomy verbs.

- Learning objectives are written in clear, learner-friendly language.
- The learning objectives are referred to throughout the lesson and progress through these is made explicit to learners. This means that learners are reminded of what they are learning and recognise their progress – this is an essential aspect of metacognition and effective assessment for learning. Some teachers find it useful to display the learning objectives throughout the lesson, either by displaying these on the board or by having them written at the top of any PowerPoint slides that are used.
- Written or verbal feedback refers to achievement against the learning objectives and recognises where these have been met and where progress has been made.

7. Quality feedback

Research has indicated that quality feedback – also referred to as formative assessment – is the single most effective thing that we can do, in schools, to help our learners make good progress (see, for example, Higgins et al. 2014). Effective feedback is also a key aspect of *Assessment for Learning* and the main way in which we support learners to understand what they need to do in order to improve and progress.

There is a huge amount of research regarding feedback and *Assessment for Learning* in general, and the research base is growing all the time. We would certainly recommend investing some time in reading and exploring this alongside your colleagues. As staff working in schools, we make a huge investment of time in giving written and spoken feedback on learners' work, and it is absolutely worth ensuring that this feedback is effective and will make a difference.

If we are honest, many of us will have experienced that nagging suspicion that, in spite of all the time we spend giving feedback about our learners' work, they do not always read/pay attention to/absorb/act on our feedback. This can be immensely frustrating, yet in many cases we plough on regardless, knowing that at least the learners' books have been marked as expected and that parents, OFSTED and SLT can see that if they need to.

We mustn't lose sight though of what feedback should really be for: quality feedback allows learners to know, understand and act on the guidance given to them about what they did well and what they can do differently next time to make it even better. The function of feedback is to inform learners about their progress so that they can learn from it and improve, and therefore make further progress. This has to include planning for them to have opportunities to really understand the feedback they are given, and also to have built-in opportunities and expectations for them to act upon the feedback until the target skills are secure. Sometimes the most effective ways of learners seeing the value of learning is by encouraging them to review the changes they have made in their work over time. This could be done in conjunction with peers, yourself or their tutor.

Given its great potential, it is vital that we consider carefully how we are going to make sure that our learners who have learning difficulties – and indeed all learners – benefit from real, high-quality feedback.

Take a quick look at the following pages for some examples of how learners might respond to the feedback we provide.

Teacher or TA	Learner response
Says to class: 'While we're waiting to begin, please can you all take a moment to read and absorb the feedback I've given you in your books.'	Thinks to himself: I can't find my pencil case … Where's Jake going to sit? I'll shout for him to come over. Oh … he's gone over there. Miss looks tired today … I wonder how long until lunch?
Has written in book: Ollie, you need to include more rhetorical questions and other persuasive devices to engage your reader.	Thinks to himself: I'll have a quick look and see what she's written … Well, for a start, I don't get what the word 'rhetorical' means, or the other long words she's put. But I can tell that she didn't think my work was any good – I must have got it wrong. I'm rubbish at English anyway.
Says to class: 'I want you all to read your feedback and make sure you do this next time.' Has written in book: Ollie, you have done really well to write in clear paragraphs like we discussed last time. It is also good that you have included some of the 'persuading' phrases that we looked at – well done! This is currently Grade F and I want you to aim for that E next time. To improve even more, I would like you to include some questions to really make your reader think.	Thinks to himself: Okay, I'll have a quick look … (three seconds later) – Right, done, read that. Shouts across the room to Jake: 'Jake, have you got a pen I can borrow?' Shouts across the room to teacher: 'Miss – Harry's got his phone out!'

Teacher or TA	Learner response
Says to learner: 'Right, I'm going to read your feedback with you and then we can check that it makes sense.' Feedback says: Ollie, you have done really well to write in clear paragraphs like we discussed last time. It is also good that you have included some of the 'persuading' phrases that we looked at – well done! This is currently Grade F and I want you to aim for that E next time. To improve even more, I would like you to include some questions to really make your reader think.	Thinks to himself: I can't believe I only got an F! I never get more than an E and everyone else is getting Cs at least. It's not even worth trying – I give up.
Says to learner: 'I'm going to read your feedback with you and we can check that it makes sense.' Feedback says: Ollie, you have done really well to write in clear paragraphs like we discussed last time. It is also good that you have included some of the 'persuading' phrases that we looked at – well done! To improve even more, I would like you to include some questions to really make your reader think. I want you to start by writing two or three questions for your reader below: _____? _____? _____?	Thinks to himself: Yep, I do understand what I need to do next. And I think she liked my work! I will have a go at writing those questions now – I have to, otherwise she'll see that the lines are still blank. Still, she's given us time to do it in so I might as well have a go.

These examples are intended to illustrate the fact that there are many ways in which the potential of feedback can get lost along the way. Some learners do not read the written feedback in their books at all, or read it but do not understand it, or read it and understand it but then move on to another topic in which the feedback is no longer relevant, and so it is forgotten.

Given the range of difficulties faced by learners with MLD in terms of memory, attention, literacy, language and mastering concepts, it is easy to see how these feedback losses are even more likely than they would be for their peers. Therefore there are additional reasons why feedback needs to be particularly well-tailored for our learners who have learning difficulties.

Furthermore, for some of our learners who have additional needs, the process of receiving feedback can feel very challenging personally. Sometimes we all see feedback as a criticism, as though the work produced is 'below par', even though we know we have tried our best and want to please others. It is important that we all feel that our efforts are accepted.

Another important factor is that written feedback is sometimes difficult for learners with learning difficulties to access – quite literally. For example, teachers' handwriting can be difficult to read, or the comments might be above the reading age of the learner, or there might be words and phrases used which are hard for the learner to understand.

There has been an expectation in recent years that learners should know their current grade or level, what they need to do to achieve the next grade or level, and that they should be able to articulate and explain these to an observer or inspector when asked. In many cases, this has led to schools giving formative feedback alongside a grade or level. This in itself is problematic though, in that it can lead to learners focusing only on the grade or level, and ignoring or overlooking the written feedback. Furthermore, for our learners with learning difficulties, this can be demotivating when their grade might be lower than that of their peers, in spite of the effort they have made.

To summarise, feedback for learners with MLD must:

- be expressed in clear language which the learner can understand;
- be specific and focused;
- link back to the key learning points, target skills or success criteria of the task;
- explain what they have done well – so they know to keep doing this!
- explain what they need to improve next;
- be understood by the learner, and include an opportunity for the teacher or TA to check their understanding;
- lead to an opportunity (ideally several opportunities – one will not always be enough) to act upon the feedback until the core skills or learning is secure.

Top ten tips for easy differentiation and personalisation

1 Know your learners. Read the SEN register and make sure you know which learners have which additional needs. Don't rely on your own impressions alone – back these up with the facts.

2 Include kinaesthetic strategies – practicals, role plays, experiments, model-making, fieldwork – opportunities to experience learning first-hand.

3 Plan for great inclusive group work – give roles and responsibilities, clear objectives, expectations and outcomes, engaging stimulus materials – and watch them fly.

4 Go round the classroom and check that learners with additional needs understand – don't assume that silence means they do. If not, explain it differently until they do. Draw pictures, show them, explain it in simpler language, act it out – do whatever it takes to help them understand. It is your job to teach them, don't give up if they don't learn the first time; use it as an opportunity to learn yourself.

5 Include picture clues to reinforce meanings of key words and ideas on worksheets and PowerPoints.

6 Keep spoken language as simple as possible. Use short sentences and explain what key words and phrases mean. Point to pictures or written reinforcements as you talk – the data projector or interactive whiteboard is great for this.

7 Present worksheets and texts clearly. Use clear and simple fonts, in at least 12 or 14 point. Try using paper in colours other than white and ask your learners which ones are easier for them. Break text up into text boxes and bullet points. Highlight key words in colour.

8 Include clearly written learning objectives, which are differentiated by level of challenge. These might include a different objective for each National Curriculum level or GCSE grade, or objectives which increase in difficulty using the verbs from Bloom's Taxonomy. Explain the objectives and make sure learners understand what they are aiming for.

9 Give quality feedback, whether written or verbal. Use clear language and always check that the learner has understood the key points. Always make sure they have a chance to act on your feedback.

10 Keep learning. Ask learners, TAs and teacher colleagues, parents and the SENCo what they feel helps the most. And be willing to share your ideas in return.

Figure 6.4   Top ten tips for easy differentiation and personalisation

8. Task analysis

There will be times when you have set a learning task or activity for a learner, and they have been unable to complete it and, therefore, to secure the skills being taught. It can be very useful to give some thought to the types of task and activity you are setting in class or in intervention so that you can pitch the task accurately.

Much of this relies on your observation of the learner in previous sessions – and this is where, if you are a teacher, you can also utilise the observations of support staff such as TAs and mentors. They are likely to have a huge amount of 'insider information' on what the learner knows/understands/is already familiar with from other lessons.

When planning an effective learning task or activity, you need to consider:

- the knowledge that learners need to already have;
- the skills that learners will need to use;
- the cognitive functions that are required for the task;
- the length of time it will take for a learner to complete the task;
- the familiarity of the task;
- the level of accuracy required.

Figure 6.5 below provides a range of frameworks which include some detailed prompts to use when analysing the demands of a task or learning activity.

If there are some learners that you know have processing difficulties, and you are giving them a task that places a lot of demand on cognitive functions, then they will need more time to work through the task than others in the class. If a task is very new, some learners may become anxious about how to approach it and so may require more time being spent explaining what they need to do and being given examples to illustrate this.

Analysing the demands of learning tasks and activities

Features of learning tasks	Questions to ask	Notes
Content or subject area	What subject or topic is the task about? What are the objectives, goals and purpose of the task? What is the learner being asked to do? How can I make this task meaningful for the learner?	
Familiarity of task/activity	How familiar or novel is the content? How familiar or novel is the vocabulary? What pre-existing knowledge and skills are necessary for the task? ■ Vocabulary? ■ Concepts? ■ Skills? ■ Experience?	
Abilities of learner required in the task	What problem-solving skills and rules does the task require? What problem-solving skills and rules do I need to teach the learner? What knowledge and skills do I need to teach the learner? Which cognitive abilities are required for the successful completion of this task? ■ Attending to the information? ■ Finding the right information? (Seeing? Hearing? Moving?) ■ Recalling previous information? ■ Explaining an answer? ■ Motivation? ■ Curiosity? ■ Knowing what they need to do? ■ Regulating their behaviour and movements? ■ Comparing items? ■ Combining information to create a solution? ■ Holding information in mind while working through other information?	

Features of learning tasks	Questions to ask	Notes
Presentation of materials – what methods are used?	Through which mode is the task presented? ■ Visual? ■ Auditory? ■ Written? ■ Kinaesthetic?	
Method of response – how is the learner expected to reply?	In which mode is the learner expected to respond? ■ Visual? ■ Auditory? ■ Written? ■ Kinaesthetic?	
Level of difficulty of the task/ activity	How complex is the task? ■ Requires only one piece of information/ process? ■ Requires two to three pieces of information/processes? ■ Requires several pieces of information/ processes? ■ Requires multiple processes or pieces of information?	
Accuracy required to be successful in the activity	How accurate do the learners need to be in the task? ■ Answers can be approximate. ■ Learners can provide their own answers with evidence. ■ Answers are either right or wrong.	
Speed required to complete the task/activity	How much time is available for the task? ■ No time limit. ■ Generous time limit. ■ Short time limit and speed is essential (e.g. quick fire round).	
Level of abstraction of task/activity	How concrete/abstract is the task? ■ The task is based on physical, real objects and ideas. ■ The task is partly based on real, physical objects and ideas. ■ The task is mostly based on abstract thoughts and ideas. ■ The task is only based on abstract thoughts and ideas.	

Figure 6.5   Analysing the demands of a task

Observation form for learners' responsiveness to adult teaching:

Teaching strategy	Not observed – may be worth trialling to see if it is an effective teaching strategy	Learner does not yet respond to this strategy	Learner responds to this strategy	Other notes
Learning intentions: The adult provides clear learning outcomes for the lesson or task to the learner				
Modality of resources: The adult uses a range of modes, including visual, auditory and kinaesthetic methods suitable to the learner's needs				
Memory: The adult uses techniques to support memory (repetition, summarisation etc.)				
Rationale: The adult provides purpose and meaning for the lesson or task				
Language: The adult pitches the lesson or task to the learner's level of language/vocabulary (including visual aids and natural gesture, if necessary)				

Teaching strategy	Not observed – may be worth trialling to see if it is an effective teaching strategy	Learner does not yet respond to this strategy	Learner responds to this strategy	Other notes
Generalisation: The adult actively encourages transfer and generalisation of learning processes from one context to another				
Pace of learning: The adult adjusts the lesson/task to the appropriate level for pace/speed				
Key aspects of task: The adult focuses the learner on important aspects of the task, e.g. pointing at key phrases				
Level of difficulty: The adult pitches the lesson/task to the appropriate level for cognitive challenge and development (not being too easy nor too hard)				
Alternative solutions: The adult encourages flexibility through exploring alternative methods to solving a problem and teaching strategic ways of answering problems				

Teaching strategy	Not observed – may be worth trialling to see if it is an effective teaching strategy	Learner does not yet respond to this strategy	Learner responds to this strategy	Other notes
Logic and critical thinking: The adult uses techniques to develop thinking through questions, testing hypotheses, requesting evidence, encouraging critical thinking				
Emotionally safe learning space: The adult creates a climate in which it is safe to make mistakes and joins the learner in their problem-solving				
Self-evaluation: The adult encourages learners to evaluate their own work				

Figure 6.6   Observation form for learners' responses to teaching

Alternative methods of recording

Where learners experience difficulties with literacy, it can seem difficult for subject teachers to assess their progress. After all, most learning and assessment of learning in schools is carried out using the medium of reading and writing, even where the core learning points relate to, for example, science, or history, or music. It can be difficult, therefore, for teachers to really get to grips with what a learner actually knows and understands, if their literacy is not at a level for them to be able to clearly communicate their ideas in their writing and if they are not easily able to access written information.

It is easy to see how literacy difficulties could become a barrier across the whole curriculum, not just in English and literacy lessons. For the learner in question, this can be very damaging indeed – particularly when they are not then able to fully access subjects where they have a relative talent. This in turn is likely to limit academic progress and enjoyment and opportunities for learning, and to reinforce feelings of low self-esteem, frustration and 'acting out' of these feelings if teachers don't find alternative ways for them to communicate their knowledge and understanding.

However, there are many ways in which staff can differentiate and personalise to ensure that literacy difficulties do not prove a barrier to progress. These are ways for teachers to make sure that the learner can communicate their knowledge and understanding and access key information and text in spite of their literacy difficulties.

There are a wide range of strategies that can be used to support learners with recording:

- access to a word processor;
- being encouraged to mind map their ideas rather than having to write in continuous prose; this can either be done on paper, or using a commercially available software package such as *Kidspiration*;
- use of a scribe, either by working with a peer or member of support staff;
- a dictaphone to record ideas;
- software which reads back what they've written, for example *Dragon Naturally Speaking*, or *Read&Write Gold*, or assistive technologies such as *Clicker*;
- writing in pairs or small groups, with designated learners taking on the role of scribe;
- scaffolded materials such as key word lists with pictures, sentence openers and writing frames;
- written feedback that focuses on content, such as understanding of key ideas and concepts, rather than literacy.

Teaching note-taking

Note-taking is a skill which learners are often expected to utilise increasingly as they progress through Key Stage 4, yet we too rarely teach our learners what good note-taking looks like, or how to decide what information is most important.

For learners with MLD, it is vital to explicitly teach note-taking. Many will find it difficult to skim and scan a page and select and process the information without specific, strategic help. They will need effective modelling of techniques for handling texts and, sometimes, constant support and reminders about the procedures they need to adopt when looking for information in books and other texts. Putting information into their own words, rather than just copying it, is a highly sophisticated language task and therefore the more scaffolding that can be provided for them, the greater the chances for them to participate fully in activities that involve them in reading to learn.

Note-taking is a crucial life skill, and one which they are likely to need in post-16 education and in the workplace. Therefore, learning how to take notes is a worthwhile investment.

Ideally, the key points of note-taking (see below for a format for this) will be taught and then can be modelled through shared note-taking before learners have a go on their own.

What is most crucial in differentiating for recording is that the staff member makes the effort and takes time to ensure that the learner knows that their needs are understood, and that there is a quality dialogue about what helps most.

It is important to remember that reducing the written expectation does not mean reducing the cognitive expectations. The cognitive elements should remain appropriate for the learner's cognitive skill.

The pages that follow provide a range of frameworks which learners can use to support note-taking in class, and to help them gather information and collate their ideas for writing.

Strategies for effective note-taking when reading

You need:

- wide-lined A4 paper, or plain paper for a spider diagram.
- coloured pens and highlighters.

Then:

- Get an overview of the text by:
  - reading the first and last paragraphs;
  - taking note of any headings, subheadings, maps, charts and diagrams.
- Make a note of the book, chapter and page for later reference.
- Prepare a spider diagram or notes sheet.
- As you read each paragraph, think about what the main idea is and note this down in just a few words.

Don't forget:

- When you write, try to:
  - shorten words when you can – 'env'ment' instead of 'environment';
  - write '+' instead of 'and';
  - leave out little words – 'the, is, to' (but do use 'no' and 'not');
  - write down names of people, places and dates.
- Copy any useful diagrams.
- Write down any new or useful words that you read.

Figure 6.7 Strategies for effective note-taking when reading

Notes on _____

Name _____

Key ideas	Useful words/ names/dates
1. _____ _____	
2. _____ _____	
3. _____ _____	
4. _____ _____	
5. _____ _____	
6. _____ _____	
7. _____ _____	
8. _____ _____	

Figure 6.8 Notes

KWL notes

This investigation will be about _____.

Name _____.

Before the investigation		After the investigation
What I know	*What I want to know*	*What I've learned*

Figure 6.9 KWL notes

QUADS notes

This investigation will be about _____.

Name _____

Question	Answer	Detail	Source

Figure 6.10 QUADS

Ideas bank

I wonder ….

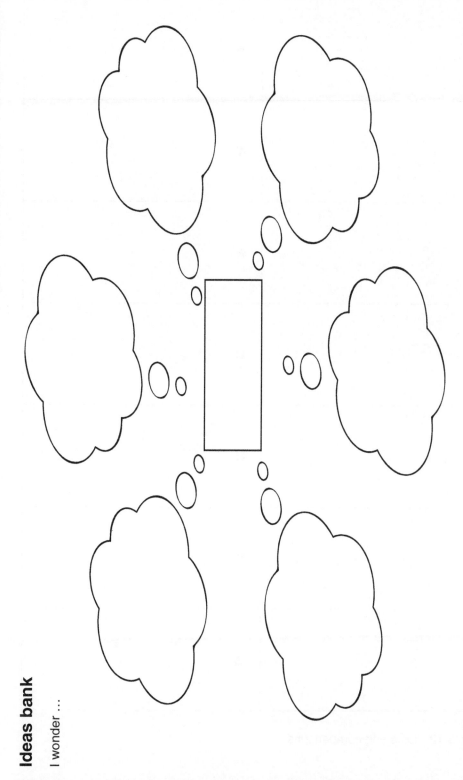

Figure 6.11 Wonder bank

Lists and comparisons

■	■
■	■
■	■
■	■
■	■
■	■
■	■

Figure 6.12   Lists and comparisons

Process planner

Name _____

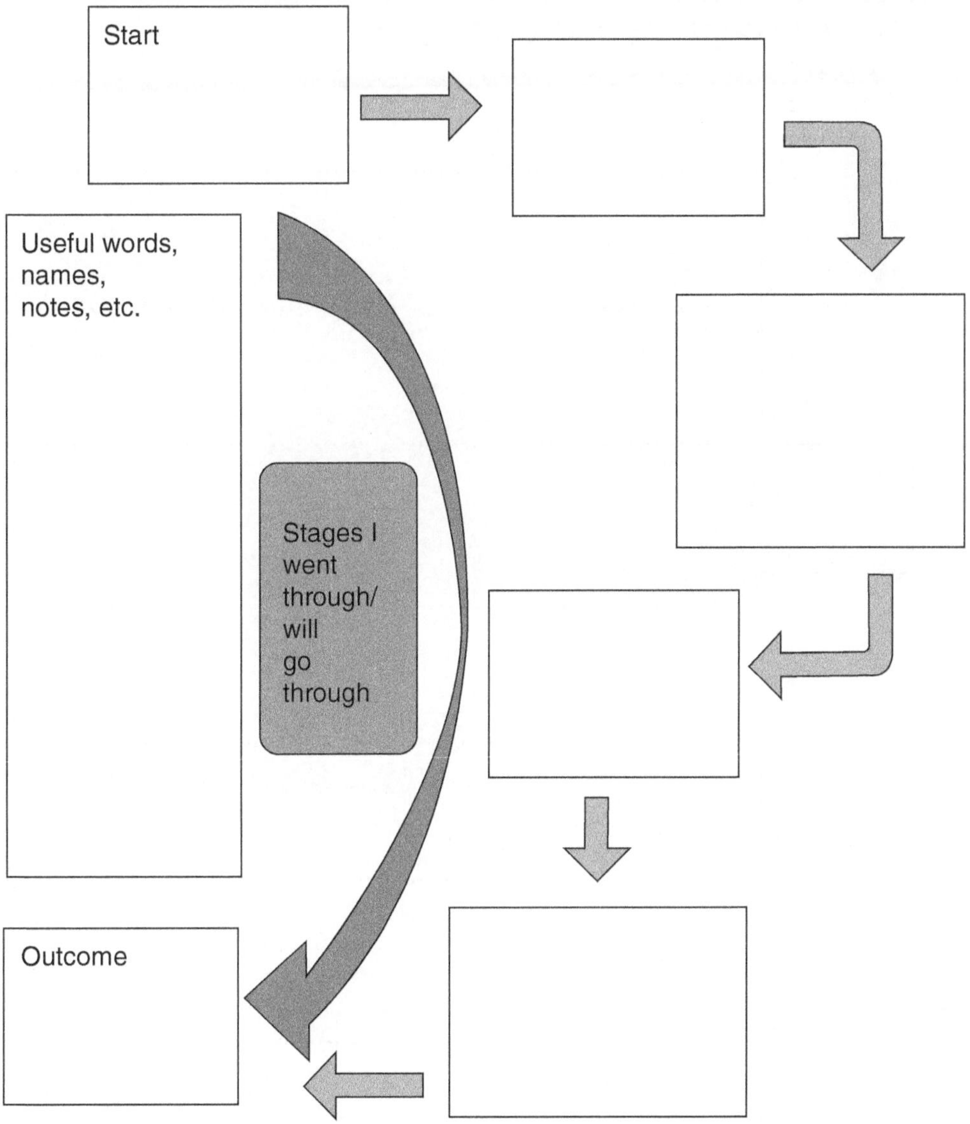

Start

Useful words,
names,
notes, etc.

Stages I
went
through/
will
go
through

Outcome

Figure 6.13 Process planner

Paragraph planning

Name _____

In the boxes, sketch or note words for the main event or idea in each paragraph. Use these when you write each paragraph.

Figure 6.14 Paragraph planning

Differentiation to improve mathematical and numeracy skills

Maths can be an area of real difficulty for learners who have MLD. Mathematical problems are often presented as numbers on the page only – so in complete abstraction, which can be very difficult to grasp without concrete materials to reinforce the ideas. There are such a large number of skills involved and that need to be combined, in order to identify a mathematical solution to a problem. In addition, learners need not only to arrive at the right solution but they also need to use the correct process and be able to present it in the appropriate way. It is easy to see why this causes more problems than being asked to write a story.

Similarly, the conceptual nature of maths can prove a barrier to mastery for many learners. They will often be able to recite number into the hundreds without actually having a secure understanding of what each number really means, what it looks like and how it relates to other numbers (sometimes referred to as understanding the 'threeness of three'). This is particularly the case where maths teachers teach number in abstraction, and fail to provide the visual and kinaesthetic props and supports that would make those numbers and number concepts come alive for learners.

So, what do we do? As mentioned earlier in the learning chapter, we need to have an awareness of how learners with MLD learn and ensure that we are teaching information and skills to an appropriate level. The first thing you need to know is what they can do. If you don't have a good baseline assessment of their core mathematical and numeracy skills then you will be 'stabbing in the dark' trying to support them. Very often we presume a huge amount yet, in our experience, it is not at all unusual to find learners who are being taught GCSE material while their number bonds to 20 or 10 are not secure.

Maths is a cumulative subject, meaning that we develop and build on what we have already learnt. This is like building a house – if we build it on unstable sand, our structure is weak and likely to fall over easily. Similarly, learners who are exposed to concepts that are beyond their level of understanding are unlikely to learn high-level skills or concepts until the underlying concepts and skills are revisited and secured. So it is vital to have a realistic and accurate picture of a learner's knowledge and skills. There are times when we are reluctant to do this because it would mean diverging from the curriculum, and we panic that we don't have time to do this. Yet in reality these learners will simply not learn unless we can go back to where they are – not just what is known, but what is actively *understood* – and start from there.

If we break maths down into the different components, we realise that number forms are only one part. In addition, we have shape, space and measure, handling data, and algebra. Learners may have one particular area of difficulty, but have a number of strengths and these can be built upon to develop the areas that are more problematic.

For the staff member who is supporting the MLD learner in maths, there are many strategies which can be used to help learners to develop their understanding of key concepts, a few of which are outlined in Figure 6.15.

Helping Maths to add up for students with learning difficulties

40 – 27 = ??

Algebra	■ Use **concrete materials** to represent the different parts of the question. These could include small empty boxes or containers to represent the 'unknown' elements. ■ Use **different coloured beads or cubes** to support learners to sort 'like' terms in an equation.
Number	■ Use **number lines** for counting on and counting backwards. ■ Use commercially available **multi-sensory systems** such as *Numicon* to support understanding of numbers and the relationships between them. ■ Use **number cubes** in sticks of different colours to represent tens, fives and units.
Shape, space and measure	■ Use **mirrors, concrete objects, nets** and **tracing paper** to show how 2D and 3D shapes are related and how they remain the same despite movement and transformations.
Data	■ Use **physical examples of charts**, e.g. pizza to represent pie chart and cut into segments. Compare terms such as quarter, half and eighths with their numerical equivalent. ■ Visually **compare graphs** and **construct real-life graphs**, e.g. pictograms using concrete objects and bar charts using cubes to represent one occurrence.

Figure 6.15 Maths differentiation

Differentiating from abstract to concrete

What is abstract and what is concrete – why does it matter what sort of information is being presented?

Concrete ideas are concepts which are based in our physical world. They are observable and measurable by using our senses:

- taste;
- touch;
- smell;
- sight;
- sound.

They enable us to get a real understanding of what it is we are meant to be learning. If we can see, touch, taste, smell or hear something it feels more real and as such we find it easier to interpret the information and hold on to it while we work with it. We trust the information and believe it to be true, therefore we can manipulate and adapt it.

In contrast, abstract ideas are ones which cannot be seen or touched. They exist in our mind as a:

- theory;
- idea;
- thought;
- feeling.

Abstract ideas exist in thought or as an idea but do not have a physical or concrete existence. It is harder to manipulate them as they don't exist in our 'real world'. Our understanding of abstract ideas builds upon our concrete knowledge, for example we know we are feeling sad if we feel like crying, or we know we are angry when we clench our fists.

Abstract ideas are more conceptually challenging than concrete ideas. Therefore, when presenting abstract ideas to learners with MLD, it is important that you give them concrete information to attach it to. For example, when learning about Pythagoras' theorem, having examples of triangles with the calculations presented reinforces how the theory makes sense.

Other ways of making the abstract concrete are:

- metaphors, analogies, and examples;
- concrete materials such as counters, blocks and writing frames;
- picture clues;
- demonstrations;
- diagrams;
- photographs;
- film.

By relating abstract ideas to concrete materials, the learner who has MLD will be better placed to develop an understanding of the target concept and to begin to make links with their prior learning.

Differentiating for the social and emotional needs of learners with MLD

One of the biggest challenges for teachers of learners within mainstream settings is managing the behavioural and social needs of learners while also ensuring the lesson is fulfilling the learning objectives. It can sometimes be difficult to ensure social integration and inclusion in the classroom, particularly when we are talking about very vulnerable learners or those who have a low level of social awareness.

Indeed, it is often asked if learners with MLD would be better suited to specialist settings, where they would be less likely to be bullied by their peers, and the honest, but often unpopular answer is no.

There is much evidence to suggest that learners who go to special schools are *more* likely to be bullied and also less likely to develop the skills that will enable them to engage as a functioning participant in their local community. That does not mean that learners who attend specialist settings are doomed, but it does mean that by 'shutting all learners with MLD away' we do not encourage the world to learn how to include them and to prosper from the skill sets that they do have.

There are, of course, some learners who are more suited to smaller teaching and learning environments so that they can develop the appropriate skills needed later in life, but most learners with MLD can be appropriately educated within our mainstream sector. As mentioned earlier, however, we may have to explicitly teach them how to acquire social, emotional and behavioural skills.

So how do we manage it and what do we do?

To meet the social needs of learners with MLD, we need to create safe learning environments for them to interact with their peers, to encounter people with different views and to develop the skills needed for appropriate social interaction. This does not require expensive interventions, but may involve games that require cooperation and a space in which to play them.

Having clear rules for these sessions is useful and can also be incorporated into the classroom – if you have a group activity have clear roles and rules for each role. Select learners based on their ability and skill set and mix up learners with needs and role-model counterparts. Social groups need good role models or else each member will learn poor social skills from the other members, who also need to develop them.

As with learning other new skills, learners with MLD may take longer to acquire these skills. Therefore, they need repeated opportunities to develop and refine social skills in different settings – small groups, whole-class settings, structured times and unstructured times. In addition, depending on the learners' needs, they may require additional considerations being made, for example to how they will understand the concept being taught and their ability to make links that may be implied rather than explicit.

Practical strategies for supporting emotional development

Emotional development is one of those areas which is felt to be vague and lacking importance; it is often overlooked by teachers as it is very abstract and hard to conceptualise. However, when it is ignored the impact is serious.

If we think back to the regulation diagram (see Figure 5.1), we see that emotional development is another aspect that needs to be taught to a learner, rather than something that they will uncover for themselves. It is important for them to develop an emotional awareness to facilitate their regulation development. A learner does not know what they are feeling unless someone tells them what it is called and what they can do about it.

A learner needs to be able to recognise what they are feeling in their body, stay focused on this long enough to reflect on what it means, and then plan how they can use this information. Otherwise the feeling is translated into action with no thought.

In our day-to-day interactions with learners, we need to teach them the signs that identify what they are feeling. We can model this to them by using phrases such as, 'You look sad, has something happened to make you feel teary?' or 'When you say hurtful things, I feel disappointed that you aren't showing me respect'. Or more generally, 'I wonder if…'. Having safe, calm spaces to explore their feelings is important and having appropriate vocabulary to differentiate between emotions is crucial.

Figure 6.16 can be used on an individual or small group basis, and as a starting point for further intervention work in this area. It provides blanks faces for the learner to write and draw different emotions. They could then compare this to their face when they feel different emotions. Mirrors can be used to show them the different facial expressions they have. If they have a basic understanding of core emotions, you can extend this by asking them how they can shift between one state and another. For example how can they move from being angry to being happy, or being jealous to being friendly? This can then be used to plan intervention to develop these areas. Encourage them to be detailed about their description of the emotions and ask them:

- Where are you normally when you feel like this?
- Who is normally around you?
- What physical characteristics do you notice?
- What are you doing when you feel like this?
- What thoughts are you having when you feel like this?
- How do you know you are feeling this?

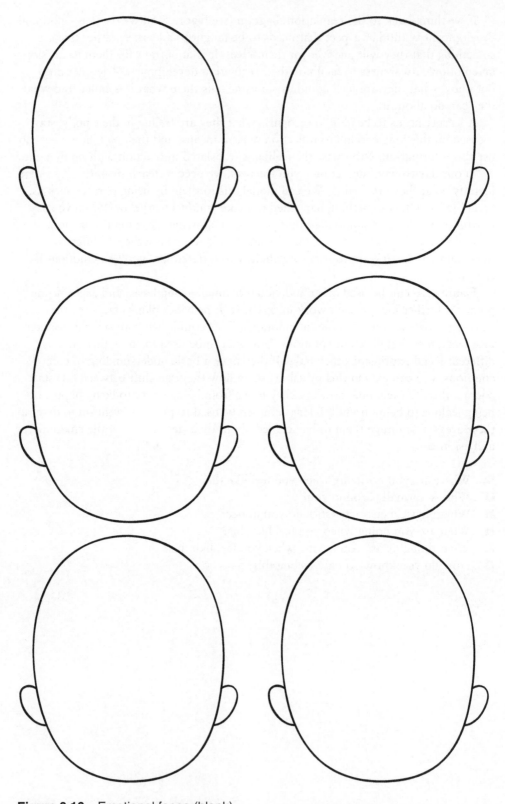

Figure 6.16 Emotional faces (blank)

Practical strategies for supporting behavioural development

Managing behaviour is simple when the basics are in place, but getting them in place requires hard work, perseverance and team cooperation. Consistency between staff members, fair punishments and consequences, recognising the positives and following through on consequences are the essential ingredients. Add to this making your lessons interesting, dynamic, practical and exciting and being a human who earns their respect, and you will enjoy the fruits of your labour.

Have strategies that make recording and noticing behaviour simple for you – for example reward charts are useless if you don't notice or record either the good or bad behaviour. You can change sad to smiley faces on a whiteboard, give ticks on a reward chart or use a three-card traffic light system to ensure that you provide the learner with clear indicators of what is expected.

The tricky part is sustaining this when you are tired and at your wit's end ... dig deep and have a spring clean on behaviour and keep the learners on their toes. Throw in an option of earning a treat or an outing if they are well-behaved and encourage the learners to monitor each other's behaviour – it is easier if you have peers encouraging good behaviour and reminding them of what they need to do.

So what are the key things to remember?

- Have a simple list of expectations and consequences – good and bad.
- Remind learners that they are making choices – good and bad – and that your job is to support them to choose the most socially appropriate one.
- *Don't* try to win the argument. Rather, let go and remember that the learner will eventually learn the hard way. This is easier said than done, but when a learner is shouting and swearing at you, seeing that you are still calm will be sweeter for you than shouting back.
- Follow through on what you say. If you give out consequences – *always* action them; follow up on things that need it. If you let poor behaviour go in the classroom, you cannot be surprised if the learners give up behaving.
- Have clear boundaries. Everyone needs to know where they stand and learners need boundaries, even if they don't like them. When they push boundaries, it is to see how flexible they are. (It is also important to note that boundaries *should* become more flexible as our learners move toward adulthood, otherwise we will have an abundance of learners living at home and feeling too scared to venture into the world of work! We need to facilitate their independence while also giving them consistency and security.)
- Get support from managers and team colleagues. Solidarity shows learners that there is agreement and a strong team behind you.
- Smile – this sounds simple but it is really hard for people to swear at you if you are smiling at them!

The frameworks that follow provide a suggestion for analysing the causes and effects of learners' challenging behaviours. The first is intended for staff to use as an observation tool, and the second is for use in reflective work with the learner him or herself.

ABC chart

Learner/group: Date/time:

Teacher: Observer:

Setting:

Day and time	Antecedents What was happening before?	Behaviour What did ... do?	Consequences What happened next?

Figure 6.17 ABC chart

Mapping behaviours

Date	Behaviour	How others felt	Consequence for me	How I felt	Instead I could have...	I would have felt ...

Figure 6.18 Mapping behaviour grid

It can be very powerful to ask the learner to reflect on their behaviour, what other people's responses were to their behaviour, what the consequence was for them and how they felt as a result of it. The purpose of this is to link external consequences and others' feelings to their feelings and behaviours – giving them a self-benefiting reason to behave more appropriately. They can also see how if they had done something different the impact for them could have been different, for example if they hadn't sworn at a teacher, they would not be in a detention, or if they had thrown a book they may have been clearing out the classroom, etc.

Over time they can look and see that when they do something undesirable – for example, swear at a teacher, there is a negative consequence and feeling for them, but when they do something appropriate they experience more positive consequences.

Maintaining high expectations of learners

Why is the focus of the new SEND Code of Practice on improving outcomes for learners with SEND? How does this fit with our view of learners with MLD as having difficulties with learning? The answer to both of these questions is because young people with learning difficulties are more able to learn than we often expect. This means that, in order to achieve their maximum potential, these learners need to be stretched more than they currently are. That is what learning is about.

If we reflect for a moment on Vygotsky's and Feuerstein's view of learning, we realise that learners are dependent on those around them to guide their learning and that they can exceed their current ability by quality teaching and mediation. That does not mean we expect all our learners to acquire knowledge and skills at the same rate, but rather that all learners need to be encouraged, stretched and challenged to go beyond their comfort zone into their Zone of Proximal Development.

In order to make this happen, we need to do what we have been discussing throughout this book. We assess, adjust and adapt constantly. This is our normal practice; the challenge is to keep reminding ourselves that our learners with MLD are constantly learning, and while it may not always be apparent, they are always able to learn more. As soon as we accept that someone is unable to learn something, we can guarantee that they will stop trying to learn it.

Ask yourself, what would I expect from a learner who didn't have a learning difficulty? What would I ask about their individual strengths, difficulties and preferences, and what adjustments would I naturally make to my expectations regarding the:

- length of time I expect them to complete the task in;
- length of time I expect them to focus for;
- amount of work I expect them to produce;
- number of times I need to go over the material in order for it to be learnt and retained;
- way I expect them to show me that they are able to use the skills and knowledge learnt?

It is vital therefore that we maintain high expectations of our learners who have MLD and keep a focus on what they can and will be able to learn with the appropriate planning and adjustment. We should never find ourselves concluding that they are unable to make any further progress – rather that we are constantly looking for ways to help them make that next vital step in their understanding.

How do we know when learning is good? Monitoring and evaluating classroom practice and management

It is very easy in schools to focus on what we are putting in to help a learner, without considering what they are getting from it. It can be very tempting to define a learner's support in terms of TA hours, additional groups, differentiated resources, additional materials and provision, without ever evaluating the impact of what is happening, how well it works and whether it is truly helpful for the learner.

We have often seen in mainstream classrooms that learners have completed beautiful pieces of work with support, without any focus on whether or not the learner understands the core concepts underpinning that work.

One learner we worked with had spent a term completing a fantastically detailed project based upon a desert island of his own devising. He had given the island a name, had planned buildings to live in and laws for life on his island, had drawn maps of the island, and had even planned a weekly menu based on what food was available on the island. With the support of his very committed TA, he had produced a project which he felt proud of and which was truly worthy of display among those of his peers.

We talked to him about his island, asking him various questions about his project, all of which he answered with enthusiasm. One question was, 'How do you think I would get to your island, if I came to visit?'. His response was, 'Miss – you could just walk there, or if you've got a car, you can drive'. What became clear was that this learner had spent a term of his English lessons producing a beautifully presented project on an island that he had created, without anyone having checked his understanding of what an island actually was.

It is crucial, therefore, that true and honest evaluation of all practice, but classroom practice in particular, starts with the learner and their understanding and progress as its central point – not with a focus on any other elements such as the work produced or the support that has gone in.

Classroom practice can be evaluated in many ways and the following are some pointers as to what this might usefully include:

- Observations of what is going on in the classroom:
  - What percentage of the time is the learner on task?
  - Is the work pitched at the right level for them to be able to work independently, at least some of the time?
  - Are they able to access key information and learning points from the lesson?
  - Do they understand what they have to do and why?

- Asking the learner key and pertinent questions to evaluate their understanding:
  - Can you tell me, in your own words, what ... means?
  - What have you learned today/this week/this term?
  - Do you know what you have to do to improve?
  - What happens in this lesson if you don't understand something?
- Additional adult support:
  - Does the support allow the learner to work towards independence?
  - How does the support stretch and challenge the learner?
  - Are the modes of support appropriate for this learner, in this lesson?
- Work scrutiny – spending some focused time analysing the work in the learner's folder or book:
  - What does the learner's work tell us about which skills they have secured, which skills are insecure and which skills are missing? What are the tiny next steps for them in this subject?
  - How often have they been able to work independently? Has the work been pitched appropriately for them to work without support at times?
  - Does their book show progress over time?
  - Are they achieving learning objectives, or do these need adjustment?
- Progress:
  - What is the evidence that the learner is making progress?
  - According to the teacher's assessment data, are they making progress over time?
  - Is this view supported by what the learner/his or her TAs/his or her family feel?

The frameworks that follow provide some starting points for reflecting on, monitoring and evaluating classroom practice across the school, within a particular subject or year group, with a focus on TA support, or for a particular learner.

These sheets are intended as the basis for classroom observation and for a follow-up chat with the class teacher or TA, and should provide a valuable 'snapshot' of how effective classroom practice is.

Framework for monitoring and evaluating classroom practice

Points to consider	Comments
Observations in the classroom ■ What percentage of the time is the learner on task? ■ Is the work pitched at the right level for them to be able to work independently, at least some of the time? ■ Are they able to access key information and learning points from the lesson? ■ Do they understand what they have to do and why?	
Asking the learner ■ Can you tell me, in your own words, what … means? ■ What have you learned today/ this week/this term? ■ Do you know what you have to do to improve? ■ What happens in this lesson if you don't understand something?	
Additional adult support ■ Does the support allow the learner to work towards independence? ■ How does the support stretch and challenge the learner? ■ Are the modes of support appropriate for this learner, in this lesson?	

Points to consider	Comments
Work scrutiny ■ What does the learner's work tell us about which skills they have secured, which skills are insecure and which skills are missing? What are the tiny next steps for them in this subject? ■ How often have they been able to work independently? Has the work been pitched appropriately for them to work without support at times? ■ Does their book show progress over time? ■ Are they achieving learning objectives, or do these need adjustment?	
Progress ■ What is the evidence that the learner is making progress? ■ According to the teacher's assessment data, are they making progress over time? ■ Is this view supported by what the learner/his or her TAs/his or her family feel?	
Other observations or comments	

Figure 6.19 Framework for monitoring and evaluating

Checklist of learners' skills

Question	Y	N
Is the learner communicating their answers in clear and concise ways?		
Is the learner comparing objects, noticing what is the same and what is different?		
Is the learner working at a reasonable pace, rather than taking a lot of time to make sure the answer is correct?		
Does the learner look for other answers, or stick with the first one that comes to mind?		
Is the learner able to explain how they solve the problem?		
Is the learner able to recall information/strategies in order to complete the tasks?		
Is the learner thinking through answers, or just guessing?		
Is the learner creating a plan to answer the question?		
Is the learner demonstrating that they understand the nature of the problem?		
Is the learner able to see when their answers are right or wrong?		
Is the learner able to reflect on their answers and the process they went through?		
Does the learner understand locations and directions, e.g. left and right, coordination?		
Can the learner transfer their learning from other problems?		
Is the learner using the correct terminology and wording?		
Is the learner seeking help and engaging with help that is offered?		
Is the learner able to keep focused for long enough?		
Is the learner able to concentrate and ignore distractions?		
Does the learner show confidence in their responses, regardless of whether they are correct or not?		
Is the learner flexible in their use of strategies in solutions they find, or are they rigid in their thinking?		
Does the learner approach problems, regardless of how difficult they think it will be?		
Is the learner keen to do well?		
Is the learner relaxed and calm?		
Is the learner willing to keep going when they start finding it hard and experience difficulties?		
Is the learner eager and alert?		

Figure 6.20   Checklist of learners' skills

Classroom Observation of Support Staff

Name of staff member: _____   Name of observer: _____

Date of observation: _____   Date of feedback: _____

	Weak Practice:	Inconsistent Practice	Good Practice:	Excellent Practice:
Professionalism:	Staff member does not sufficiently meet expectations for professionalism and role-modelling e.g. ■ Rarely positive or respectful towards students, the organisation, families, colleagues ■ Does not model good punctuality – often late to classes ■ Does not consistently carry or use correct equipment to support key students ■ Does not wear suitable professional dress ■ Does not show proactive or supportive behaviours towards students and colleagues	Staff member demonstrates some expectations for professionalism and role-modelling but these may be inconsistent or varied e.g. ■ Sometimes positive and respectful towards and about students, the organisation, families, and colleagues ■ Does not always model good punctuality –sometimes late to classes ■ Does not consistently carry or use correct equipment to support key students ■ Does not consistently wear suitable professional dress ■ Does not consistently show proactive or supportive behaviours towards students and colleagues	Staff member consistently demonstrates expectations for professionalism and role-modelling e.g. ■ Actively positive and respectful towards and about students, the organisation, families, and colleagues, regardless of challenge or difficulties ■ Models excellent punctuality ■ Carries and always uses correct equipment to support key students ■ Wears suitable professional dress ■ Proactive and supportive of students and colleagues	Staff member consistently demonstrates and exceeds expectations for professionalism and role-modelling e.g. ■ Actively positive and respectful towards and about students, the organisation, families, and colleagues, regardless of challenge or difficulties ■ Models excellent punctuality ■ Carries and always uses correct equipment to support key students ■ Wears suitable professional dress ■ Exceptionally proactive and supportive of students and colleagues
Modes of Support:	Staff member provides support in the classroom but relies on one or two modes of support, regardless of student need.	Staff member provides support in the classroom but usually relies on a limited repertoire of modes of support, regardless of student need.	Staff member employs appropriate modes of support in the classroom. These may include, but are not limited to, support with generating ideas, 'getting started', facilitating group work, monitoring from a distance etc. These are mainly tailored effectively and sensitively to situation and need.	Staff member sensitively employs a wide range of appropriate modes of support in the classroom. These may include, but are not limited to, support with generating ideas, 'getting started', facilitating group work, monitoring from a distance etc. These are tailored and selected effectively according to situation and need.

Professional Expertise:	Staff member is not familiar with the needs of his or her core student/s and is not able to describe: ■ Their level of need ■ Their category of need ■ Their strengths ■ Their current targets ■ Their target grade or level ■ Their current grade or level	Staff member is not familiar with the needs of his or her core student/s and struggles to describe: ■ Their level of need ■ Their category of need ■ Their strengths ■ Their current targets ■ Their target grade or level ■ Their current grade or level	Staff member is familiar with the needs of his or her core student/s and can describe: ■ Their level of need ■ Their category of need ■ Their strengths ■ Their current targets ■ Their target grade or level ■ Their current grade or level	Staff member is familiar with the needs of his or her core student/s and can confidently describe: ■ Their level of need ■ Their category of need ■ Their strengths ■ Their current targets ■ Their cognitive ability (e.g. referring to CATS or other data) ■ Their progress this year to date ■ Their target grade or level ■ Their current grade or level
Supporting towards Independence:	Staff member provides support which prevents the student/s from enjoying independence and inclusion in the lesson. This may include, but is not limited to, sitting next to them throughout the session, acting as their partner instead of a peer, scribing for them throughout when they could write, etc.	Staff member tailors support so that the student/s is/are able to enjoy some independence and inclusion in the lesson.	Staff member tailors support so that the student/s is/are able to enjoy a good degree of independence and inclusion in the lesson.	Staff member tailors support so that the student/s is/are able to work to his or her own optimum level of independence and inclusion in the lesson.

Summary of areas of strength identified and discussed:	Summary of targets set and discussed:
Date set for review:	Signed Staff member: Observer:

Figure 6.21 Classroom observation of support staff

Chapter 7

What next? Next steps, summary and conclusions

Transitions and endings

It is vital that we always remember that our learners will have a life beyond the classroom and beyond our schools. Within just a few short years, they will be forging ahead with their own lives; in many cases attending college, seeking employment, forming new friendships and relationships, and becoming increasingly independent. We should never forget, in our work with our learners, that an independent and happy life is the ultimate goal – this is the 'best life' that we talked about earlier in this book. With this goal in mind we need to make sure we invest time and quality planning in ensuring smooth and effective transitions at post-16.

The key here is to always be thinking about the outcomes they need to have achieved for the transition into the next stage of their life. Where is all the learning they are doing actually taking them? By backtracking from the desired end point, you can plan the learning and skills they need to do or gain along the way. This needs to be done in conjunction with the learner and their parents, if appropriate.

All too often, we see learners leave primary or secondary school without the necessary skills for the next chapter in their learning and our response is, 'Well, they are not ready, we should keep them back or send them to a safer place'.

Instead of this approach, we need to have discussions with colleges, sixth-form staff, employers and learners about what they need to be doing to enable them to be successful some time before they are about to leave. We need to think about life skills, competencies and qualities that are fundamental for independence and ensure these are also focused on through a learner's time at school.

We can't take for granted that learners will just *know* how to do such crucial things as:

- feeding themselves and cooking;
- managing money;
- travelling around;
- attending interviews;
- making choices;
- staying safe in public and online;
- cleaning and maintaining clothes.

Learners with MLD will need opportunities to be taught these skills. It may be that they are put in touch with clubs and organisations that can help with this, or it may be something that needs to be offered at school. This needs to be considered well in advance of the transition itself.

Conversations also need to happen with colleges and sixth forms well before learners think about applying for college, apprenticeships and so on, to discuss what skills are required and how handovers will be conducted to ensure continuity. This is the responsibility of the secondary school and it may be in some settings that this work is commissioned to be delivered by a specialist external provider.

In either case, learners can benefit from an overlay of support, in which there is a period of time in which both sectors are involved before and after transition. This is more effective than moving between two completely discrete packages of support, and means that the appropriate support can be seamlessly delivered across the period of transition.

Summary and conclusion

In this book, we hope to have provided an introduction to the understanding and support of learners with moderate learning difficulties in the secondary school. We have presented an outline of the background to inclusive practice and clarified why it is everyone's responsibility. We have explored how people learn and why this is relevant. We have clarified the range of skills that learners need in order to be successful and how these can be developed when they need to be. We have also presented some general strategies for differentiating work within the classroom.

The new SEND Code of Practice is clear that learners with special educational needs and disabilities require quality teaching, and when this is in place learners will make appropriate progress. For those learners who are not making progress, teachers are still responsible, along with the SENCo, for providing appropriate interventions and adaptations within the classroom.

Learners with MLD can make good progress; they just require adaptations to be made to the mode of presentation, the mode of response and the volume of information given to them. As supporters of teaching and learning, it is right that we should expect *all* learners to make progress and this is equally true of learners with MLD. We need to have clear outcomes for them and these need to feed into the next chapter of their learning journey. We are always learning; it is a lifelong process, and as practitioners within the education system, we can lead the way by modelling learning and listening to our learners. This is our unique and vital role through the work we do, and in the book we have demonstrated some practical and concrete ways in which all learners can access their entitlement to a quality and inclusive education.

Further information, references and recommended reading

On capturing learners' views and person-centred planning

Spyrou, S. (2011) The limits of children's voices: From authenticity to critical, reflexive representation. *Childhood* 18(2): 151–165.

Stephenson, A. (2009) Horses in the sandpit: photography, prolonged involvement and 'stepping back' as strategies for listening to children's voices. *Early Child Development and Care* 179(2): 131–141.

United Nations (1990) Convention on the Rights of the Child. Available from http://www2. ohchr.org/english/law/crc.htm

United Nations (2008) Convention on the Rights of Persons with Disabilities. Available from http://www.un.org/disabilities/convention/conventionfull.shtml.

On differentiation and inclusive strategies in the classroom

Norwich, B. and Jones, J. (2014) What have we learned? What are the future prospects and ways forward? In B. Norwich and J. Jones (eds) *Lesson Study: Making a Difference to Teaching Pupils with Learning Difficulties*. London: Bloomsbury.

Vlachou, A., Didaskalou, E. and Argyrakouli, E. (2006) Preferences of students with general learning difficulties for different service delivery modes. *European Journal of Special Needs Education* 21(2): 201–216.

On inclusion

Alliance for Inclusive Education: http://www.allfie.org.uk/

Barton, L. (1988) *The Politics of Special Educational Needs*. London: Falmer.

Cigman, R. (2007) *Included or Excluded? The Challenge of the Mainstream for some SEN Children*. Abingdon: Routledge.

Clark, C., Dyson, A., Millward, A. and Robson, S. (1999) Theories of inclusion, Theories of schools: deconstructing and reconstructing the 'inclusive' school. *British Educational Research Journal* 25(2): 157–177.

Equality Act (2010) London: The Stationery Office.

Gross, J. (2002) *Special Educational Needs in the Primary School: A Practical Approach, 3rd ed.* Maidenhead: Open University Press.

Kenny, M., Shevlin, M., Noonan Walsh, P. and McNeela, E. (2005) Accessing mainstream: examining the struggle for parents of children who have learning difficulties. *Journal of Research in Special Educational Needs* 5(1): 11–19.

Lewis, A. and Lindsay, G. (2000) *Researching Children's Perspectives.* Buckingham: Open University Press.

Lewis, A. and Porter, J. (2004) Interviewing children and young people with learning disabilities: Guidelines for researchers and multi-professional practice. *British Journal of Learning Disabilities* 32: 191–197.

OFSTED (2006) *Does It Matter Where Pupils Are Taught? Provision and Outcomes in Different Settings for Pupils with Learning Difficulties and Disabilities.* OFSTED HMI 2535.

Oliver, M. (1990) *The Politics of Disablement.* London: Macmillan.

Paliokosta, P. and Blandford, S. (2010) Inclusion in school: a policy, ideology or lived experience? Similar findings in diverse school cultures. *Support for Learning* 25(4): 179–193.

Phelps, A. and Hanley-Maxwell, C. (1997) School to work transitions for youth with disabilities: A review of outcomes and practices. *Review of Educational Research* 67(2): 197–226.

Roaf, C. and Bines, H. (1989) *Needs, Rights and Opportunities.* Exeter: Falmer Press.

Slorach, R. (2011) Marxism and disability. *International Socialism* 129. Available at http://www.isj.org.uk/index.php4?id=702&issue=129 (accessed 21 January 2012).

Swain, J. and French, S. (2008) *Disability on Equal Terms.* London: Sage.

On learning

Baddeley, A. D. (2000) The episodic buffer: A new component of working memory? *Trends in Cognitive Sciences* 4(11): 417–423.

Baddeley, A. D. and Hitch, G. J. (1974) Working memory. In G. H. Bower (ed.) *The Psychology of Learning and Motivation (Vol. 8).* London: Academic Press.

Deutsch, R. (2010, October) Cognitive Assessment Profile training presented at the Winter Gardens, Weston-super-Mare, North Somerset.

Feuerstein, R. (1983) *Instrumental Enrichment.* Baltimore: University Park Press.

Feuerstein, R. and Jensen, M. (1980) Instrumental enrichment: Theoretical basis, goals, and instruments. *The Educational Forum* 44(4): 401–423.

Haring, N. G., Lovitt, T. C., Eaton, M. D. and Hansen, C. L. (1978). *The Fourth R: Research in the Classroom.* Columbus, OH: Charles E. Merrill Publishing Co.

James, W. (1890/2000) *The Principles of Psychology Vol. 1.* New York: Dover Publications.

King, S. and Saxton, M. (2010) Opportunities for language development: Small group conversations in the nursery class. *Educational and Child Psychology* 27(4): 31–44.

Mentis, M., Dunn-Bernstein, M. and Mentis, M. (2008) *Mediated Learning: Teaching, Tasks, and Tools to Unlock Cognitive Potential.* California: Corwin Press.

Piaget, J. (1959) *The Psychology of Intelligence.* London: Lowe and Brydone.

Seifert, T. and O'Keefe, B. (2001) The relationship of work avoidance and learning goals to perceived competence, externality and meaning. *British Journal of Educational Psychology* 71: 81–92.

UK Assessment Reform Group (1999) *Assessment for Learning: Beyond the Black Box.* Available from www.nuffieldfoundation.org/sites/default/files/files/beyond_blackbox.pdf

Vygotsky, L. (1978) *Mind in Society.* Cambridge, MA: Harvard University Press.

Wood, D., Bruner, J. S. and Ross, G. (1976) The role of tutoring in problem solving. *Journal of Child Psychology and Psychiatry* 17(2): 89–100.

On moderate learning difficulties

Algozzine, B. and Ysseldyke, J. E. (1986) The future of the LD field: Screening and diagnosis. *Journal of Learning Disabilities* 19(7): 394–398.

DfES (2003) *Data Collection by Type of Special Educational Needs*. London: DfES.

Dockrell, J. and McShane, J. (1992) *Children's Learning Difficulties: A Cognitive Approach*. Oxford: Blackwell.

Farrell, M. (2006) *The Effective Teacher's Guide to Moderate, Severe and Profound Learning Difficulties (Cognitive Impairments)*. Abingdon: Routledge.

Greenspan, S. (2006) Functional concepts in mental retardation: Finding the natural essence of an artificial category. *Exceptionality* 14(4): 205–224.

Norwich, B. (2004) *Moderate Learning Difficulties and Inclusion: The End of a Category?* Presented at British Educational Research Conference, Manchester 2004.

Norwich, B. and Kelly, N. (2005) *Moderate Learning Difficulties and the Future of Inclusion*. London: Routledge.

Kelly, N. and Norwich, B. (2004) Pupils' perceptions of self and of labels: Moderate learning difficulties in mainstream and special schools. *British Journal of Educational Psychology* 74: 411–435.

Torgesen, J. (1986) Learning disabilities theory: Its current state and future prospects. *Journal of Learning Disabilities* 19(7): 399–407.

Westwood, P. (2004) *Learning and Learning Difficulties: A Handbook for Teachers*. London: David Fulton Press.

Ysseldyke, J. E., Algozzine, B., Shinn, M. R. and McGue, M. (2001) Similarities and differences between low-achievers and students classified learning disabled. *Journal of Special Education* 16(1): 73–85.

On special educational needs and disability

Department for Education (2011) *Teachers' Standards: Guidance for School Leaders, School Staff and Governing Bodies*. London: DFE (DFE-00066-2011).

Department for Education (2014) *Statistical First Release: Special Educational Needs in England: January 2014*. London: DFE (SFR 26/2014).

Department for Education and Department of Health (2014) *Special Educational Needs and Disability Code Of Practice: 0–25 years. July 2014*. London: DfE and DoH (DFE-00205-2013).

OFSTED (2010) *A Statement Is Not Enough: The Special Educational Needs and Disability Review*. OFSTED 090221.

OFSTED (2015) *School Inspection Handbook: Handbook for Inspecting Schools in England under Section 5 of the Education Act 2005 (as amended by the Education Act 2011)*. OFSTED 120101.

Warnock, M. (1978) *The Warnock Report on Special Educational Needs*. London: The Stationery Office.

On support and intervention

Alborz, A., Pearson, D., Farrell, P. T. and Howes, A. J. (2009) *The Impact of Adult Support Staff on Pupils and Mainstream Schools*. London: EPPI-Centre.

Blatchford, P., Russell, A., Bassett, P., Brown, P. and Martin, C. (2007) The role and effects of teaching assistants in English primary schools. *British Educational Research Journal* 33(1): 5–26.

Blatchford, P., Bassett, P., Brown, P., Koutsoubou, M., Martin, C., Russell, A. and Webster, R. (2009a) *Deployment and Impact of Support Staff in Schools*. Research Report DCSF-RR148.

Blatchford, P., Bassett, P. and Brown, P. (2009b) *The Effect of Support Staff on Pupil Engagement and Individual Attention*. Research Report DCSF–RR154.

Blatchford, P., Russell, A. and Webster, R. (2012) *Reassessing the Impact of Teaching Assistants*. Abingdon: Routledge.

Brooks, G. (2012) *What Works for Children and Young People with Literacy Difficulties? The Effectiveness of Intervention Schemes*. Berkshire: Dyslexia-SPLD Trust.

Giangreco, M. F., Edelman, S. W., Luiselli, T. E. and MacFarland, S. Z. C. (1997) Helping or hovering: Effects of instructional assistant proximity on students with disabilities. *Exceptional Children* 64(1): 7–18.

Glenny, G. (2005) The ethics of intervention. *Support for Learning* 20(1): 12–16.

Higgins, S., Katsipataki, M., Kokotsaki, D., Coleman, R., Major, L. E. and Coe, R. (2014) *The Sutton Trust–Education Endowment Foundation. Teaching and Learning Toolkit*. London: Education Endowment Foundation.

Tennant, G. (2001) The rhetoric and reality of learning support in the classroom: Towards a synthesis. *Support for Learning* 16(4): 184–188.

White, G. S. (2010) Balancing acts in the half-way houses: The role of resourced provisions in mainstream schools. *British Journal of Special Education* 37(4): 175–179.

Index